Rags and Riches

Make My Day – Book 26
Larry M. Henares, Jr.

Published, February 2018

Dr. Hilarion M. Henares Jr., known as **Larry Henares,** is a graduate of Ateneo de Manila, University of the Philippines, and the Massachusetts Institute of Technology, an engineer, economist, educator, big businessman, writer, civic leader, public servant, and hobbyist (guns, books, amateur radio and electronics).

He is a writer known for his essays on economics, history, art and culture, a front page columnist in the pre-martial law Manila Times and the most widely read column in the Philippines, according to all surveys, the daily "Make my Day" in the Philippine Daily Inquirer, after the EDSA revolt.

ooooo

Tatay Jobo Elizes, Self-Publisher

This book is published under permission of

DR. HILARION M. HENARES, JR.

This permission is subject to withdrawal any time so desired, in which case, **Tatay Jobo Elizes,** as self-publisher will cease publishing this book. LARRY HENARES is free to republish with other publishers. Tatay Jobo disclaims any responsibility for writings of the Author. Printing of this book is using the present day method of Print-on-Demand (POD) system, where prints will never run out of copies.

ISBN – 13: 978 - 1985745988
and ISBN – 10: 1985745984

No part of this book may be reproduced or copied in any form without written permission from Larry Henares, and Tatay Jobo Elizes. Contact; job_elizes@yahoo.com Websites: http:www.tinyurl.com/mj76ccq

Ooooo

About the Book,
"RAGS AND RICHES"

In this Book 26 of the Make My Day series, Henares chronicles how he started making home movies, Hollywood style, based on his first born son's favorite stories, St. George and the Dragon, and Noah's Ark. He could not find a knight's costume, so he used a cowboy's costume and re-christened the hero, Hopalong St. George. He could not build an Ark, so he used a banca, and called the movie Noah's Act, gets the nursemaid to represent Noah's Family, and a pet dog to represent the Animals, and himself as the rest of the sinful human race who deserved to drown because he would not say his bedtime prayers, nor eat his breakfast properly, nor brush his teeth, and whose dying words were "Give me a toothbrush so I can save myself!" A 50 feet roll of Kodachrome cost a fabulous P50, and will only run 3 ½ minutes, so the epic St. George and the Dragon filmed to run 2:35 minutes; and the epic Noah's Act was compressed to a mini-epic 2:12 minutes! The unused film footage was incorporated into Henares' third film, based on his own favorite story, The Tell-Tale Heart, which run for 3:32 minutes, and which was such a horror story, it caused nightmares for the rest of the children generations hence.

The rest of the Shadows on the Wall featured a surfeit of good Filipino movies that came much later, many of them starring Larry Henares' favorite ex-future daughter-in-law Vilma Santos. This included the OTHER Golden Age of Filipino Cinema during Martial Law (since it was the only way to protest against the dictatorship, and to take advantage of Imelda's tolerance for bold sex films). A critic (not Henares) observed that there were no good films in the time of Cory Aquino, whose only two contributions to the film industry were Censors chief "moral hypocrite" Manoling Morato, and an "appallingly untalented" aspiring-actress daughter Kris Aquino, hahaha.

On Stage, Henares chronicles the magic moment when the musical giant Ryan Cayabyab and La Môme Celeste Legaspi shared the same stage "to restate an eternal truth -- to distill the soul of a nation -- to crystallize the hopes, fears and aspirations of a people -- and bring forth the good, the beautiful and the common humanity of all men." And the divine spark of pure goodness that creates such artists as RJ Jacinto and Jose Mari Chan, music-makers, dreamer of dreams, movers and shakers of the world.

Then he tells us of a new book by cartoonist Frank Miller, "The Dark Knight Returns" about Batman, long a two-dimensional comic strip, now transformed into a four-dimensional bundle of neuroses, using computer-generated graphics. The book is a phenomenal development in the art of comics, a new approach to graphic story-telling that dealt with adult themes full of intensity, passion and power. It was a historic coming of age of a beloved art form.

The rest of this book is pure Henares, detailing the shenanigans of people in power: Gethsemane of Alran Bengzon; Seventh Heaven of Bobby Borja who grows bougainville vines on Meralco's power lines and anticipates pushing up daisies after a thunderstorm; the $500 million project of George Marcelo, a village subdivision made of styropor on top of the sea, using alternative renewable power sources; Jaime de la Rosa with a brother named Rogelio, who is not a movie star, and the mess he made in the Food Terminal Inc.; Perils of Eggie Apostol and the Philippine Daily Inquirer; the epic struggle and lonely battle of Rep. Tet Garcia against foreigners and the palace cronies.

Then he writes of the foreign policy in crisis, the covert war waged against us by Malaysia, about homosexuals, about pyrrhic victories worse than defeats, about Justice above all though the heavens fall, and about the Doctor YES, the doctor of the future.

Good reading of the Henares style of writing, that enlightens, inspires, educates, astounds, delights, amuses, and imbues us with a sense of childlike wonder. Enjoy.

ooooo

BOOK 26: RAGS AND RICHES

TABLE OF CONTENTS

SHADOWS ON THE WALL

1. How Our Home Movies were filmed

As a toddler I grew up in the barrio of Tinongan, in the municipality of Isabela, in the province of Occidental Negros, where my father was a sort of Chief Engineer in charge of developing supplementary products from the waste of Isabela Sugar Central for the Montilla owners, courtesy of my maternal grandfather Don Daniel Maramba, the Grand Old Man of Pangasinan.

There was a movie theater behind our house, set up for the entertainment of the employees, which showed nothing but silent motion pictures.   At the time talking pictures were not yet developed, and the silent movie was in its golden years.

At the time, Tom Mix, Tom Tyler and Hoot Gibson were the cowboy stars, but a dog star named Rin-Tin-Tin beat them all in popularity and remuneration. Greta Garbo, Gloria Swanson and Clara Bow were the great female stars and Rudolf Valentino, Douglas Fairbanks and John Barrymore were the great male stars. Mickey Mouse and Betty Boop were the cartoon stars.

I started going to watch movies at the age of 2, and became a movie addict till now. My favorites then were Douglas Fairbanks who starred in *Three Musketeers*, *The Mark of Zorro*, *Don Q the Son of Zorro*, *The Thief of Baghdad* – with acrobatics better than any modern action star – and Rudolf Valentino who starred in such epics as *The Four Horsemen of the Apocalypse*, *Blood and Sand*, *The Eagle*, *The Sheik*, and *The Son of the Sheik* – with torrid love scenes, and great battle scenes.

Fast forward to the 1950s, I bought a movie camera, got married and begot a son, Ronnie my first-born, all of which were filmed in a home movie called *From Here to Maternity*, a pun on the Oscar-awarded film, *From Here to Eternity*.

My Kodak camera used 8 mm Kodachrome with 10 ASA at 16 frames per second, and had the problem of parallax, which cuts part of the scene offscreen. Parallax is a phenomenon that occurs because the viewer is located a few inches from the lens, and does not see the picture exactly as the lens does. Through-the-lens viewing solved the problem several years later. The 50 feet roll of film cost P50, expensive at the time, and gave me only 3.5 minutes running time. Most of my early home movies depicted scenes of our family life – picnics, parties, and babies being coaxed to stand up, walk and smile. Nothing could be more boring to our family and friends. Why not film movies Hollywood style, of the favorite stories of our son? asked my wife Cecilia. And Ronnie's movie career was launched.

What are your favorite stories, Ronnie? The little boy, only three years of age, answered: St. George and the Dragon and Noah Ark. And these were the first two movies we filmed., and they were a sensation! And you Larry, what is your favorite story? asked Cecilia. I said, The Tell-Tale Heart by Edgar Allan Poe. And that was third movie we made.

I went shopping for a knight's costume with shield and sword, and a dragon to kill; couldn't find any to buy. I was going to Hong Kong to shop for some, but my wife objected. Larry, use your imagination, Cecilia said, make it into a cowboy movie as Hopalong St. George. I made the movie, but I could see in Cecilia's eyes a glimmer of inspiration to make children's costumes as a business, and the idea of HENLICH was born.. The name sounds German which my wife had one-fourth blood, but it is really a combination of Henares and Lichauco.
November 1, 2017

2. HOPALONG ST. GEORGE AND THE DRAGON

First the title and the credits: starring 3-year old Ronnie as Hopalong St. George, his mother Cecilia as the Damsel in Distress along with baby brother Atom in a crib as prop, and his father Larry costumed in pajamas and a Halloween mask, gloves and shoes. as the Dragon, and a rocking wooden horse as his faithful steed. The play lasted exactly 2:35 minutes.

Ominous horrendous footsteps on the grass.
Gnarled hand on the knob of the front door which opens.
Damsel with a baby, turns around and screams.
Horrible face of the Dragon in close-up.
Close-up of Damsel's face screaming
The Dragon attacks and screams and the struggle continue.

Scene shifts to Hopalong St. George on his horse strolling by. He hears the screams and speeds to the rescue, the trees and scenery sweeping by in his wake (we contrived this with an improvised merry-go-round).

In front of the house, St. George gets off his horse, rushes up the stairs, opens the front door and rushes in.

The Dragon lets go of the Damsel. Turns around to confront the new threat.

Hopalong St. George attacks and the fight is on. St. George knocks the villain down, gets up a chair, jumps on him, and pummels him. Finally. he pulls his gun out and shoots the Dragon. The Dragon goes down. He shoots him again, and again. And a couple of shots as coup d'grace.

Hell, we did not know how to get rid of the corpse, and time and the film was running short. So…

Scene shifts to the Damsel in distress. Embracing and kissing our hero for saving her and the baby. But kissing is for sissies, so St. George extricates himself says Goodbye, leaving the Damsel crying and waving at the doorstep.

Hopalong St. George rides off into the sunset on his faithful steed, strumming a guitar and singing "Don't Fence Me In!"

The End.

We added sound later, synchronizing with a tape recorder, the musical background, the sound effects, the screams, and the cowboy song. sung by Gene Autry.

3. NOAH'S ACT

It took a lot of imagination to make this epic story into a mini-epic, but we did it!

First the title, all illustrated, and the credits: Ronnie Henares as Noah; his teen-aged Nursemaid Nora as his Family; his pet dog Pooch representing all of the animals; a Banca representing the Ark; and the houseboy Andy (half shown) as Jehovah, steadying the banca while creating the waves; a garden hose to spout the rain; an umbrella to shield Noah and Family from the rain; the swimming pool as the Flood; co-starring his father Old Man Larry Henares in his twenties, playing the rest of the sinful world population. The film lasted only 2:12 minutes. *Color by MC Paints* (which my factory manufactured).

The scene opens in the bedroom where Noah kneeling before the crucifix, saying his evening prayers, while the Old Man screams Baloney! I don't believe in God! Stop it! Let's go to sleep!

The next scene is in on the dining table with Noah and the Old Man having breakfast. Noah is dutifully eating his cereal, milk and eggs, while the Old Man refuses to eat, throws his napkin on the table, and storms out, screaming, I won't eat this crap! I'm going out to buy me a lollypop and ice-cream!

Scene shifts to the bathroom where Noah dutifully brushes his teeth, while the Old Man screams I don't care if I have tooth decay, I won't brush my teeth, and throws his toothbrush away.

Noah wags his finger at him saying Hala galit ang Dios sa iyo! God will punish you because you don't pray, you don't eat properly, you don't brush your teeth! He points to the crucifix, the room darkens and a lightning bolt lights it up!

The rains fall on the ground, on the Old Man, till he stands ankle deep in water. Then knee-deep in the ensuing flood.

In the meantime, Noah and Nora -- his Family -- and the dog Pooch -- his menagerie -- under an umbrella, are ensconced in the banca – his Ark – Andy as Jehovah steadies the banca during the storm…

The Old Man screams Oh my God! Oh my God! as the rains lash at his face!

Neck deep in the flood, he screams to Noah, Give a toothbrush! Give me a toothbrush so I can save myself!

Noah gallantly extends his hand to give him a toothbrush! Too late, too late! The stormy sea overcomes the Old Man, and he drowns! Serves him right!

The End.

We added the musical background and the dialogue later on a tape recorder and synchronized it with the film.

4. THE TELL-TALE HEART

First the title and the credits: JOVIBOY CRUZ in EDGAR ALLAN POE'S… *a naked heart being skewered by a dagger,* flash the title – THE TELL-TALE HEART… and the movie proceeds with Joviboy (aged 5) as the killer, my adoptive brother, Miguel Villanueva (aged 8) as the Policeman, and Larry Henares (in his 20s) as the Victim with a Halloween mask.…

The Killer cringing against the wall, his fevered mind imagining the eyes of the Victim on him. He covers his eyes and screams, Oh my God he wants to kill me! Oh no! He uncovers his face, and cringes, Those eyes! Those eyes! His left arm wards off the danger, his right hand lifts a dagger and strikes!

Strikes again and again and again in slow motion.… The blood drips to the floor, drop by drop while a heartbeat is heard louder and louder and louder, and then stops!

The killer is then seen replacing the floorboards to cover the body of his victim underneath, and nailing them back to the floor. I killed him, I killed him, and I am hiding his corpse under the floor where nobody will ever find him!

A hand knocking repeatedly on the door.

The killer startled, looks up. A policeman opens the door. The killer welcomes him, asks him to sit down on a chair, saying What can I do for you. Officer?

The Policeman answers, I am here to investigate, the neighbors claim there were screams coming from this house!

That is not true, Officer, answers the killer, I had the radio on, perhaps that is what my neighbors heard.

Well that explains everything, the Policeman said, I guess I will be leaving now. He stands up.

No! No! protested the Killer, Stay a while and have a cup of coffee. Thanks, I like that, he said, and the Killer pours the coffee into the cup and hands it to the Policeman.

The Policeman fumbles, and the coffee spills on the floor. Drop, drop, drop, with the heartbeat drumming louder and louder into the killer's fevered brain.

So sorry, so clumsy of me, exclaimed the Policeman..

But the killer was not listening, his eyes were transfixed on the dropping water and the heartbeat louder and louder, as the drops of water merges into drops of blood, the heartbeat louder and louder.

The policeman was laughing at his own clumsiness, and his laughter joins the beat of the tell-tale heart

Ha ha ha, drop, drop drop, beat, beat. beat – the Killer cowers, he claps his hands to his ears, the beat of the tell-tale heart thunders on! Finally his brain explodes, THERE! There under the floorboards, I buried him! I killed him! I killed him!

The Killer beats his head against the wall, while the Policeman lifted up the floorboards, and there is revealed the gory and mutilated body of the Victim!

The Killer faints.

An Henares Presentation, THE END, color by MC PAINTS

Pardon the article "an", but Henares is pronounced with a silent H, like NRS. The movie lasted only 3:32 minutes and was a true masterpiece, thanks to Joviboy's acting. This damned movie brought nightmares to my Ronnie, his siblings, his cousins and his friends. I did not know this till years and years later. I am sorry, really I am.

5. What movies were like in the days of old

My grandson Quark Henares was a Palanca Awardee at the age of 19 and a movie director at the age of 20. When at the age of 26, he finally met this famed director Quentin Tarantino, he knelt before his idol and told him that at the age of 12, he decided to be a movie director when he saw Tarantino's *Pulp Fiction*. Tarantino responded by saying that he viewed Quark's movie *Keka*, and pronounced it a masterpiece. Both Quentin and Quark spent hours together just being bull-sitting friends. I tell this story because Quark most certainly inherited from me his love for movies, and I want to tell him about the movies of old.

I was a movie fan for as long as I remember, and I can tell you that all my life I rarely paid to see a movie. My parents when I was a student, my friend Anding Roces whose father owned Ideal Theater, MTRCB which issued me passes, and Mayor Binay whose senior citizen's card assured us of free access to Makati theaters – all subsidized my movie addiction. I am 83 years old now and I saw a movie at least 3 times a week for all of 81 years. I have seen all the eight versions of the Three Musketeers from Douglas Fairbanks Sr. to Gene Kelly. I have seen all the Charlie Chaplin movies, of which *City Lights* and *Gold Rush* were the best. I have seen all the masterpieces of Eisenstein (*Battleship Potemkin*), of D. W. Griffith (*Birth of a Nation*, *Intolerance*), de Mille, Capra, Lubitsch, Hitchcock, and the new ones too.

The movies went through a period of uncensored license especially during the silent days and the early talkies, and was finally forced to regulate itself through the Hays Office and the Catholic Legion of Decency. What were movies like in the good old days?

First, kisses were performed discreetly with closed lips, no French kiss or open mouth allowed. No man and woman were allowed to lie in one bed, even if they were husband and wife. No pregnant belly allowed even just before giving birth. Breasts may be thinly veiled but no breastfeeding of babies allowed; all babies were bottle-fed. A cowboy did not kiss his girl, he just rode off into the sunset with his horse.

Second, guns were never aimed steadily with two hands; guns were brought into action with one arm brought down like a karate chop and fired. And when the gun ran out of bullets, it was stared at with surprise and thrown away in disgust at the man it was supposed to shoot. The West must have been littered with guns thrown away after the first six bullets were fired. All fights, even street rumbles, were conducted like a boxing match under the Queensbury rules, no kicking, no chopping, no kneeing in the groin, no elbowing, no tripping – martial arts were unknown to movies till after World War II. All Indians were considered savages and cannon fodder, and are killed off like buffalos by the cowboys with impunity. All Negroes are depicted as ugly, stupid and lazy, good only as servants and comic relief. Most Asians were depicted as uncivilized despots and sex obsessed villains.

Third, in every movie home there was the ubiquitous bar where drinks were served, the most startling of all being the omnipresence of ice cubes at any time, whether in the dead of night or in the early hours of the morning – without anyone ever explaining how they got there, since the drinkers just entered the house. Ghosts or robots as butlers?

Before the war, cars drove on the left side of the road, and Catholic school days were off on Thursdays and Sundays. Thursday was our movie day; we had the whole city to ourselves. Thursday was when the weekly movie program changed, and second-run theaters exhibited chapter-plays and double film shows, with a little vaudeville live show thrown in. Jeepneys were unknown then, and were called jitneys or auto-bus. In movies of old, gay meant happy, queens wore crowns, queer meant different, grass was what horses ate, cocks crowed, pussies meowed, and there were no such words as shit, piss, fuck, tits, penis or vagina. Believe it or not.
December 24, 2007

6. At last a good Filipino movie

I call myself a nationalist, yet I detest Filipino movies. I have seen the best, *tinimbang ngunit kulang. Kulang talaga.* The action films are phony, they cannot even contrive a believable karate fight or a car chase or a fire explosion or anything. Sex scenes do not affect the groin, the violence does not touch the nerve endings. The story line does not challenge the mind or the imagination. The best of them are pale copies of foreign movies, and seeing Peque Gallaga's imitation of *Gone with the Wind's* burning of Atlanta only made me snicker, his cutting off of hands and tearing of of face made me puke. And every time I see this fellow genius and *kasinmanwa* from Negros, my only thought is to wish he would get a good haircut and a long hot bath.

Lamberto Avellana is too arty and too slow. Lino Brocka is too arty, and is obsessed with the seamier side of life that leaves no room for concern or sympathy, only disgust. Danny Zialcita and Gerardo de Leon are masters of fast paced editing and the intercut, and I really enjoy their films, only I cannot remember even the movie title five minutes after I leave the theater. Manny de Leon's son's movies leave me cold, they are so contrived I could not laugh or cry. I actually walked out of a movie made by Armida PE SR's son when I saw my friend Armida, old, ugly, unkempt and *uli-anin*, picking rice off the floor. How a son can do that to his own beautiful mother is reprehensible. His portrayal of Rosanna Roces as a bitch was phony, she couldn't even make my manhood rise to the occasion.

I love my ex-future daughter in law Vilma Santos, but her movies are the worst I have seen, even the ones that involved my son Ronnie. Believe it or not, I stayed in the car reading while my driver watched Vilma's movie with a transceiver, calling me to come in just in time to see Ronnie dance with Vilma. And only Vilma movie I could tolerate up to now is the one she made with Nora Aunor under the direction of Danny Zialcita, where both had a homosexual relationship that made me vomit.

I call myself a nationalist, but I think that Filipino movies are pure unmitigated shit. They are too slow, too long, too haphazardly done, each scene milked to the dregs *ad nauseum*. Most of the screen characters are caricatures. In all my life I have been watching and hoping that some Filipino genius would make a truly great Filipino film comparable to Satyajit Ray's Apu Trilogy, specially *Pather Panchali*, and give us one moment of sheer beauty with rain drops falling on a young girl's face, a memorable scene that still sticks to the mind and brings tears to the eyes 40 years after I saw it last. Or one comparable to Kurosawa's portraits of a lonely Japanese bureaucrat (*Ikiru*) and a tough but kind-hearted doctor (*Red Beard*). Something that touches the heart.

Yesterday I saw one Filipino movie that touched my heart. It was directed by the son of my friend Jose Rono, entitled, "*Bata, Bata, Paano Ka Ginawa?*" which I translate for my American friends Dick Gordon and Dick Romulo as "Child, child, how were you made?" A great performance by Vilma Santos as a single mother of two children born of different fathers: Ariel Rivera, an actor of great sensitivity, and Albert Martinez who tends to overact. And two child actors, one of whom, the daughter (Serena Dalrymple), practically stole the show. At long last a good Filipino movie!

Bata, Bata, Paano Ka Ginawa?

Woman is such a complex complicated creature that it takes a great artist to delineate her personality. Leonardo da Vinci did it with the stroke of the brush with his painting of Mona Lisa. Honore de Balzac did it with the stroke of a pen in his book Cousin Bette. The women in William Shakespeare's plays are so unique (Lady Macbeth, Portia, Juliet, Kate) yet so true to life, they haunt you 400 years after they were created. Movies gave us memorable characterizations of such women as Scarlet O'Hara, Ninotchka, and Tolstoy's Anna Karenina. And probably for the first time in Philippine movie history where one-dimensional cardboard stereotypes of women abound, a real believable character emerges: the portrait of the woman Lea in the Chito Roño's *Bata, Bata, Paano Ka Ginawa*.

Lea, played in an award-deserving performance by Vilma Santos, is a middle aged mother of two children, one boy, one girl, sired by two different fathers. She was married to the first, Ariel Rivera, but was separated from him when he left to work in Surigao. She decided to stay in Manila because she felt she had her own life to lead. He asks, "Do you ever regret having loved me?" And she answers, "Of course not, you gave me my child, didn't you?"

He is now married to another woman with a newly born baby. When he says goodbye to her as he is to embark for another job in the United States, Lea, now abandoned by her boyfriend, asks him plaintively, her eyes pleading, "May I borrow you for just one day? We can visit old familiar places, and order bibingka like we used to, and be silly once again." The next scene was Lea and Ariel naked in bed in a motel, and they were both sobbing softly. Oh miracle of miracles, no interminable scene milked dry to the dregs, no embellishments, no hysterics, no unnecessary talk – only a woman and her man, embracing each other, with silent tears for their lost love, their lost youth, and their lost years.

Her boyfriend, played by Albert Martinez, father of her daughter, has a mother who refuses to have anything to do with Lea. He does not show up on Christmas, as promised to the daughter, and Lea embarrassedly covers up, "It is only New Year, December is a long way off." Then he does show up as she was putting away the Christmas decorations. "Let's talk," he says and she answers, "Please let us not quarrel" and in a conciliatory tone, "I have a new set of New Year's resolutions." He gives her the bad news, "I am leaving you. I just got married to another." She continues with her packing, stunned and trying to hold back her tears. "Do you understand what I am saying?" asks the boyfriend, and she explodes with a cry of pain and anger that wrenches your heart.

There is this scene with a co-worker, played by Raymond Bagatsing, when Lea suddenly blurts out, "Make love to me. I often wish that in the act of love, a man's penis will reach deep and touch my very soul, probing the secrets I dare not utter." In scene with another co-worker, a nun, Lea teases her, "Don't you ever wonder how it is to be loved by a man?"

When the two fathers invite their children to come away with them, leaving their mother, in tears they plead, "Help us decide," but with breaking heart, she tells them they must make their own decision, that she will always be their mom.

For sometime the school principal (Rosemarie Gil) has been patronizing Lea, the single parent, advising to give her two children just one name Bustamante, her maiden name, instead of naming them after their respective fathers, because it confuses those who know they are siblings, and of course to hide the fact that there are two men in her life. Lea refuses to take away their rightful names. One day she casually mentions that she was working for a NGO with Catholic nuns to care for "Women in Crisis." The principal stammers, "I thought you were a hospitality girl," and a new respect shines in her eyes. After learning of the wonderful work Lea does with abused mothers and abandoned children, the principal invites Lea to be guest speaker for "Women's Day."

On the eve of Women's Day, the two children approach their mother to tell her they decided to stay with her, with a cake in celebration, "Happy Women's Day." In the school convocation, Lea stammers, "When my son was small, he used to ask me how he was made (echoing the title of the movie). Today he never asks anymore so I assume he already knows. But I believe the more important question is how to make our children better citizens of a better world, how to make them reach for the stars!"

And that's the point of the movie: how a strong-willed woman comes to terms with her fate, and how she imparts her strength of character, her independence of mind, her integrity as a human being, to the children she loves.

This is my pecker, this is for fun!

When Vilma Santos, then a teenage movie star, fresh from being miscast as Imee Marcos in a political propaganda film, went to Las Vegas to pay her respects to Frank Sinatra, Old Blue Eyes cupped her face with his hands and softly said, "You are beautiful, baby." Vilma Santos, my ex-future daughter in law is indeed a beautiful girl, and it is nice to see her grow gracefully into middle-age like my son Ronnie. Nice indeed to see her star in a movie I consider one of the best movies of the Filipino film industry, "*Bata, Bata, Paano Ka Ginawa?*" It is certainly the most intelligent and most mature Filipino movie I have ever seen.

The story comes from a prize-winning (Palanca Award) novel by Lualhati Bautista, and the direction by Chito Roño is restrained and executed with great respect for the material. Above all, the performance by Vilma Santos is superb. Like Meryl Streep's, her every expression is a work of art. Exasperation: her boyfriend holds two eggs for cooking, "What do I do with these?" and she answers, "Damn it, make them into chickens!" Disgust: "Trouble with men, they think their penis is made of gold, and they use it to terrorize women. Like those soldiers in the movie Full Metal Jacket who chant, 'This is my weapon, this is my gun, this is my pecker, this is for fun.'"

Having been called stupid for not remembering which of her two men did not bring her to the hospital when she was about to give birth, she exclaims: "Stupid? Stupid? That what's I am for having anything to do with the two of you!" And a hint of resignation creeps into her statement: "It is good to be sad sometimes, it makes happiness all the more of value." And that moving scene with her son who refused to be a boy scout because he did not have a father to hang a neckerchief on him, "I can do all that for you. I can be your father too. Please do not blame me for something your father could not do."

But her best scenes are those where she does not say a single word, and her face spells volumes: a beautiful smile that radiates pure happiness, silent tears that speak of a lost youth or a pending loss of loved ones moving away, sighs of relief that whisper through a forest of frustrations like a fresh breeze, outbursts of pain and anger that wrench and scorch our hearts, a blank face awaiting the end of a loveless lustful copulation, a heartful empathy with the tragedies of others played out before her eyes, and eyes begging, reaching out, just reaching out for a little compassion, a little love.

It is Vilma's scenes with her young child, Maya played by Serena Dalrymple that really fascinates the audience, the interplay and interaction between mother and daughter in which Serena practically steals every scene. This naughty spunky child bursts into the movie at the very beginning with a hilarious piece rendered in a school contest of how she was born (echoing the title of the movie). Then while her parents stand aghast, she explains to her classmates and their parents, "God did not have anything to do with it. My mother was married to the father of my brother by a city judge. My father married my mother in bed." And those spats with her brother about which of their fathers their mother loves, and Vilma is forced to answer, "Both! I love them both! By God, love is not division, it is multiplication. Elizabeth Taylor had seven husbands, and she loved them all."

But Serena's best scenes occur when she is making chismis, or asking embarrassing questions, or bursting out in tears over problems she could not understand and over which she has no control. We parents recognize in her our own little daughter, that loveable little scamp that is the heaven in our lives.

October 2, 5, 7, 1998, ISYU

7. Pebble on the Sand

Bato sa Buhagin is a movie starring Vilma Santos and Fernando Poe Jr. The story is that of a spoiled rich girl (played by Vilma) who is told by a fortune-teller that within 3 days, she will bump into the man who will be the love of her life. Driving her car, she bumps into a taxi driven by Fernando Poe. Though the accident is her fault, she contrives to have Poe fired from his job. Knowing this and to avoid a lengthy court case, her father gives him a job as the driver for his spoiled daughter, who without knowing it, suffers from a dread disease, probably leukemia, from which she will eventually die. Teased by her friends about the possibility that a mere driver Poe might be the love of her life, Vilma makes his life miserable, treating him as a fool and an inferior. While she drunkenly berates and humiliates him in front of her friends, she collapses and is taken to the hospital, where the doctor tells her father that her end is near. She realizes what a monster she has been and apologizes to Poe, and slowly she begins to fall in love with him. At the end, she asks him to take her out sightseeing. Feeling so weak, she has to lean on him for support. It was then that she tells him that she knows the secret that her father has kept from her, that she is dying. She collapses and falls into his arms, and in despair, cries out for the first and last time, "I love you!" And he answers, "I love you too." She whispers, "When I am gone, do not weep for me! Wherever I will be, I'll wait for you," and dies in his arms. He carries her away, while the song Bato Sa Buhagin plays on the sound track... the scene shifts to the funeral, attended by her family and her friends, while Poe stands apart and far away from her, as befits a mere driver, turns around and walks away as the song ends, and the credits appear on the screen. The End.

My beautiful computer expert Rachel David was on hold on a phone call from Malaysia where she is working. I was singing aloud the song from the film and translating it to English. When I took the call, I heard her crying copiously online, *"Nakakalungkot, napa iyak ako!"* That title song on the theme of unfulfilled love, won the FAMAS award for the best theme song of the year. Let me sing it for you:

Bato Sa Buhangin
Kapag ang puso'y natutong magmahal
Bawat tibok ay may kulay at buhay
Ngunit kung ang pagsuyo'y lilipas din
Bagay kaya ang Bato sa buhangin?
Kay hirap unawain bawa't damdamin
Pangakong magmahal hanggang libing
Sa langit may tagpuan din at doon hihintayin
Itong bato sa buhangin.

And the translation in English, as I understood it from the movie, is as follows:

Pebble on the Sand
When the heart learns to love,
Every heartbeat acquires color and life.
However, if love becomes impossible and prematurely ends for
 us on this earth,
Can a pebble be in harmony with the sand on which it lies?
How hard it is to understand such feeling --
For if we swear to love one another beyond the grave,
Surely, there must be in heaven a place for us to meet,
And there I will wait for you,
Like a pebble lying on the sand.
September, 2014

8. Sarah and KC compared

Time was when I could declare truthfully that "My love of country ends where my distaste for Filipino movies begins." In all my 76 years before the Third Millennium I never enjoyed a Filipino movie, except two -- "*Paa Ng Kwago*" directed by Gerardo de Leon, and "Jaguar" starring Nora Aunor and Vilma Santos directed by Danny Zialcita. These two potboilers were tightly scripted, intercut and intelligently directed, without the slow pace and tendency to milk scenes for tears that characterize the work of our "great" directors.

Then I saw "*Magnifico*" a wonderful movie about a little boy with a heart of gold, one of the very best movies I have ever seen. This was followed shortly after by "*Keka*" very funny story about a female serial killer, directed by my grandson Quark Henares. Both were wonderful.

Recently I was in Vicky Belo's 18th Anniversary Celebration, where three singers were invited to sing: Lani Misalucha, Regine Velasquez and Sarah Geronimo. I was used to the first two who were once managed by my son Ronnie Henares. The third one, Sarah, had a strong voice in a small frame, was not particularly good-looking, and did not impress me much. But that was before I saw her first movie.

Every Friday, I take out my secretary, my driver and my maids for lunch and a movie. I have gotten a little sick and tired of foreign blockbusters that send my mind reeling over computer-generated action, so I asked my guests to select the movie we were going to watch. They all selected Filipino movies. The first was a flick with a very intelligent script, "When Love Begins" starring Aga Mulach as an environmentalist in Boracay. The second was "Caregiver" a well-scripted and beautifully acted movie starring Sharon Cuneta in Great Britain. The third was "A Very Special Love," starring Sarah Geronimo and John Lloyd Cruz. The fourth was "For The First Time" starring KC Concepcion and Richard Gutierrez in Greece. I hate to do this, but I have to compare Sarah and KC, in what appear to be their initial film offerings. Especially since both involve the same story line – adult children belaboring under the heavy expectations of their elders.

The first instant I saw Sarah Geronimo in the movie, I fell in love with her. That pug-nosed little twerp loomed larger than life on the big screen, luminous and beguiling. How can I explain that? Her eyes, oh those eyes, she is the only one of two actresses (the other is Nora Aunor) who could emote with her eyes. That one scene when Lloyd (with his 5 o'clock shadow) was speaking to his staff, with his face inches away from hers, and her eyes looking at every facet of his face, with such love and longing! And that momentary panic in her eyes when alone with her, Lloyd sternly asked her to close and lock the door, just before he continued, "after you leave the room." And that "rain dance" of hers, which she performed with dancing eyes, is a movie classic. I chuckle many times in fond remembrance of it. Thanks to the scriptwriter and director.

Considering that her parents have been training and saving her for this film debut, KC, to be frank, was a disappointment. To begin with, she is a trifle too overweight, with a face and girth too large to match Richard's slim figure. She is a beautiful girl, but it rarely showed on the screen, the director and the cameraman being not too choosy about camera angles, and her wardrobe an absolute disaster. And the most memorable scene of hers is her big ass slung over the shoulder of Richard, farting, making *otot* continuously. It was not even funny. The script is unintelligent and rang false. The role of Richard as a good-looking roué who still maintains good relations with his ex-girlfriends and their husbands, is unbelievable – my three sons are like that and they don't merit a hello from their ex's. The only one in my family who is in good terms with her ex-boyfriends and their wives is Elvira, and that is because she is unspoiled and unselfish. In the movie, Richard is anything but unspoiled and unselfish. The movie venue could have been anywhere, but having chosen Greece, it takes an idiot of a scriptwriter not to include the Parthenon in one of the

scenes. As for motivations, KC's father seemed like a psycho with a reverse Oedipus Complex; Richard's retreat from love cannot be explained adequately by a brief dialogue with a disappointed lover. On the other hand, take John Lloyd Cruz's utter failure in his own company, his humble application for a job as his elder half-brother's assistant, and his brother's rising and shaking Lloyd's hand, saying, "Welcome to the family firm. You've changed a lot for the better. Whoever or whatever made you change is worth keeping." To me that was a wonderful, neat and off-beat resolution of a sibling rivalry, and of the love between boy and girl. The last scenes of the two movies, involving love-play between Sarah and Lloyd on one hand, a KC and Richard on the other, are worth comparing.   The former was delightful like two gazelles at play, the latter pathetic, like an elephant and giraffe in combat.
November 5, 2008

9. The Other Golden Age of Philippine Cinema by Noel Vera

When we talk about the Golden Age of Philippine Cinema we often mean the '50s, with artists like Manuel Silos, Manuel Conde, Lamberto Avellana, and Gerardo de Leon, or (and more often) the '70s, with artists like Lino Brocka, Ishmael Bernal, Celso Ad. Castillo, Mario O'Hara, Mike de Leon.

The problem is that golden ages, like any other cultural and social movement, rarely follow calendar dates. The dawning of December 31, 1979 didn't mean the conditions and talents that created the great films of the '70s suddenly vanished -- if anything, conditions persisted, and some of the artists from the previous decade did their best work in the next one.

Perhaps not in the case of Lino Brocka. Brocka in three incredible years, from 1974 to 1976, would direct the three greatest Filipino films in contemporary cinema: *"Tinimbang Ka Ngunit Kulang"* (You Were Weighed and Found Wanting, 1974), *"Maynila sa Kuko ng Liwanag"* (Manila in the Claws of Neon Lights, 1975), and *"Insiang"* (1976). He would still be active in the '80s, but by about this time Brocka discovered politics, and (or so the theory goes) it ended his career as an artist. *"Bayan Ko"* (My Country, 1985), and *"Orapronobis"* (Pray for Us, 1989) are not much more than political agitprop; excellently made and highly effective agitprop, but compared to something like *"Insiang,"* which criticizes Philippine society in a subtler, more complex, more dramatically intense level...

Ishmael Bernal, on the other hand, would sound off the start of the decade with his masterpiece, the epic "Manila By Night" (1980). The film has aged a little; visually it has nothing on Brocka's *"Maynila Sa Kuko"* (brilliantly shot by Mike de Leon), and the city onscreen looks actually cleaner and more livable than it is today. But the sheer nastiness of the characters, the corrosive nature of life in Bernal's underworld, the overall nihilism of the work -- tempered by the artist's unnervingly cool distance towards his material -- is still a wonder to behold.

Bernal was active for the remainder of the decade. His '80s output -- in terms of range, variety, overall quality -- rivaled (some would say bested) Brocka's: the hallucinogenic *"Himala"* (Miracle, 1981); the sparely realist *"Relasyon"* (Relationship, 1982); the painfully honest "Broken Marriage" (1983); the quiet, intense *"Hinugot sa Langit"* (Wrenched from Heaven, 1985 --incidentally, one of the finest films ever about abortion).

One filmmaker who came into his own in the '80s is Mike de Leon. In the mid-'70s he was both producer and cinematographer of Brocka's *"Maynila sa Kuko"*; he also directed the memorably gothic *"Itim"* (Black, 1976). From 1980 to 1982, however, he made a trilogy of films that many consider his best work: *"Kakabakaba Ka Ba?"* (Worried? 1980), *"Kisapmata"* (Blink of an Eye, 1981) and "Batch '81" (1982). "Kakabakaba" is sophisticated satire (perhaps too sophisticated) with a distinctively designed look. "Kisapmata" is a simple horror story about a pregnant daughter and her overbearing father but one so powerfully made (I think it's the best film he's ever done), it became a metaphor for many things: the Marcos dictatorship; the oppressive dominance of men; and de Leon's own dark, twisted sensibilities. "Batch '81," about school fraternities, is more clearly an allegory on fascism; if it's a step down from *"Kisapmata,"* that may be because it's difficult to improve on a great and perfect film.

Golden Age of Bold Films

De Leon would go on to make the overrated "Sister Stella L." (1984), his one nod to fashionable liberal politics, and the underrated *"Hindi Nahahati ang Langit"* (The Heavens Indivisible, 1985), his one fascinatingly subversive attempt at adapting "*komiks*" material (about a young man and his unaccountably intense attraction to his half-sister) to the big screen.

Mario O'Hara, like Bernal and Brocka before him, would make his "Manila" movie -- three of them: "Condemned" (1984); "*Bulaklak* ng City Jail" (Flowers of the City Jail, 1985), and "*Bagong Hari*" (The New King, 1986). O'Hara's "Manila Trilogy" represents a range of genres (from noir to drama to action) and social milieu (from street hustlers to women convicts to an alternate-reality vision of Manila) that few Filipino filmmakers have even approached in terms of sweep and intensity.

Finally, the '80s were nothing if not the Golden Age of the Filipino "bold" film. These were erotic films that, for one reason or another, the Marcos dictatorship had allowed to be made -- had, in fact, encouraged, through funding from the Experimental Cinema of the Philippines, and through uncut screenings at Imelda Marcos' Manila Film Center. The rational? Who knows? Perhaps the Marcoses were too engrossed in other troubles (the Aquino assassination; the devaluation of the peso; the swelling opposition movement). Perhaps they wanted to show the world that they were more liberalized, more enlightened. Perhaps they encouraged sex flicks to distract the general public -- a kind of desperate bid to give them what they want, "bread and circuses" style.

Whatever the underlying cause, the effect is a blooming of erotic flesh, photographed in a variety of storytelling styles, often by newcomers to the industry who are either doing their debut features, or have done them not too long ago. Of the better ones I might cite Abbo de la Cruz's "*Misteryo sa Tuwa*" (Joyful Mystery, 1984) a somewhat sadistic fable on the evils of money; Chito Rono's "Private Show" (1986), a *noir* on live-sex performers; and William Pascual's "*Takaw Tukso*" (Temptation, 1986), a Bergmanesque chamber piece written by Armando Lao. Three others I would consider not just the three best Filipino erotic films ever made but three among the '80s' best: Tikoy Aguiluz's "Boatman" (1984), also about live-sex performers, but with Aguiluz's unique documentary style; Peque Gallaga's "Scorpio Nights," a no-holes-barred film about a student screwing his downstairs neighbor's wife; and Laurice Guillen's "*Init sa Magdamag*" (Midnight Passion 1985, script by Racquel Villavicencio), about a woman drawn, willingly or unwillingly we aren't sure, into a sadomasochistic relationship. Mention should be made of an extraordinary debut that was neither erotic nor mainstream; it wasn't even a full-length feature. "*Ang Magpakailanman*" (The Eternity, 1983) is a twenty-minute short written, directed, and photographed by Raymond Red, about a mysterious book of the same title and the young man searching for it. The film has more wit, originality, and visual imagination than a dozen lesser Filipino features; and though Red will eventually do what Brocka, Bernal, and de Leon failed to do -- become the first Filipino to win the Palme d'Or in Cannes with his short "Anino" (Shadows, 2000) -- this remains his real masterpiece.

During Cory's time, no good films

A final note: two films stand out amongst an amazing array of greats and near-greats – Gallaga's "Scorpio Nights" and O'Hara's "*Bagong Hari*." Both expressed the nihilism and despair of the Filipino people in the waning Marcos era – "Scorpio Nights" with its breathtakingly death-defying sex, "*Bagong Hari*" with its relentlessly violent depictions of death. Both, literally, were the last words on the last years of the Marcos era; there's an almost terminal aura about them, as if anything more said -- on sex, on violence, on everything in between -- would only be redundant. With impeccable timing, the month after "*Bagong Hari*" closed on its opening day on January, 1986 (it was a commercial disaster), the EDSA Revolution overthrew the Marcos dictatorship --making "Bagong Hari" the last great film of the '80s, and (arguably) of the " '70s Golden Age of Philippine Cinema."

After February 1986 – nothing, literally nothing. Marcos' successor, President Corazon Aquino, was no friend -- not even a good influence -- on the local film industry (there's joke going around that Aquino's two great contributions to Philippine cinema was Censors chief and moral hypocrite "Manoling" Morato and her appallingly untalented aspiring-actress daughter, Kris Aquino). The only significant Filipino production made from 1987 to 1989, in fact, was Lino Brocka's "Orapronobis" -- which was made with French money and which accuses Aquino of being even worse than Marcos, the way a weak leader with little or no control over her administration is worse than a dictator. It wouldn"t be until 1995 -- nine long years -- that anything even resembling a recovery would appear in the distance.

I must confess that I am not an enthusiast of Filipino films, avoiding them as much as I can. In my opinion, they are generally very bad copies of bad American movies. Even the best of them are slow-paced, belaboring every point, milking every scene, as if to point out how stupid and beetle-brained our Filipino movie audiences are. There has never been a real original masterpiece among the Filipino movies I have ever watched. No Akiro Kurosawa, no Fellini, no Bergman, nothing, zero among our Filipino directors.

The first Filipino movie I ever enjoyed watching was *Paa ng Kuwago*, directed by Dr. Gerardo de Leon in the 1950s. It was tightly edited, no redundant or superfluous scenes, the intercutting dictating the pace of the movie right up to the climax of the horror movie. Truth to tell, I did not enjoy the subsequent movies directed by Gerry de Leon, specifically his so-called masterpieces, the *Noli Mi Tangere* and the *El Filibusterismo*. They followed Rizal's novels too closely, with too many side stories that detract from the main story line, none of the sweep and grandeur one associated with Victor Hugo's novels which Rizal wanted so much to emulate.

Between you and me, Lamberto Avellana and Lino Brocka, the two most honored directors of Philippine movies, were too concerned with social issues, and too enamored of the Italian *Verite* directors to develop a really good motion picture that can hold the interest of a movie buff like I am. There is one other director who is good in editing tight and fast paced scenes, and that is Danny Zialcita who made a good movie with Nora Aunor and Vilma Santos.
December 16-18, 2002

10. 'Superfan': The gay behind Ate Guy, by Meryll Yan

Before Manny Pacquiao and even before Judy Ann Santos and Sharon Cuneta, there was one person who epitomized the word "idol" and that was actress Nora Aunor. Nora is the Filipino dream made real. Plucked from a life of poverty and obscurity and thrust into the stage, she started collecting singing trophies at the age of 11 and later won in the *Tawag ng Tanghalan* show. The rest, as they say, is history, and the chocolate-skinned, plain-faced girl would rewrite all the showbiz rules and go on to become the Superstar.

Philippine showbiz may have already produced a constellation of talents, but none can yet rival the Superstar, or Ate Guy as she is fondly called by her supporters. Many a biography has been done on the great Nora Aunor, but none yet to feature her most loyal devotee, Mandy Diaz. That is, until now. Thanks to Clodualdo "Doy" del Mundo Jr., the pen behind iconic films *Maynila sa mga Kuko ng Liwanag*, *Kisapmata* and *Merika*, Diaz now gets to tell his story.

Superfan, the latest digital short film written, produced and directed by Del Mundo, recounts the life of Diaz, the number-one fan of the Superstar. It is only fitting that the Superstar would have an equal-wattage fan in the person of Diaz. If Aunor started her career at 11, Diaz began his fandom when he was in Grade 1. If Aunor endorsed Coke, Diaz drank Coke. If Aunor had a movie out, Diaz would be the first to watch it. Even in his deathbed, Diaz forbade his friends from burying him if Aunor did not visit his coffin.

Diaz did not live in a parallel universe with Aunor. His universe was Aunor. Having started his obsession with Aunor at a very young age, Diaz would eventually accumulate a priceless collection of Aunor memorabilia -- magazine covers, gowns, vinyl records and everything else Nora. It is not surprising that he would become the walking encyclopedia of Aunor's life and career. In *Superfan*, del Mundo re-imagines the life of Diaz, who is ably fleshed out by in the film by veteran thespian Nonie Buencamino.

How did del Mundo channel Diaz's spirit? "I read Mandy's essay, 'Himala,' about his life as a Noranian, and I also interviewed his partner and his fellow Noranians," recounts del Mundo, and thus resulting in the words for Buencamino to deliver.

Since Diaz's life revolved around Aunor, watching *Superfan* is like taking an audio- visual trip down Aunor's career. Clips from classic Aunor movies complement Diaz's retelling of his life. The film even includes a bit of cheek on the Nora Aunor versus Vilma Santos rivalry. If Aunor was the Filipino Cinderella, then Diaz was her self-styled fairy gaymother.

Humor aside, Diaz's story is really that of a life offered to the service of his idol. Del Mundo wisely describes the protagonist, "A fan manifests behavior that is irrational. You cannot explain it." Through the character of Diaz, we see fame from the point of view of the admiring rather than the admired. And in him, we see an extreme, but true, version of ourselves -- ordinary people who live vicariously through the bigger, shinier lives of our extraordinary idols. Although Diaz has already passed away, the mania is still alive as proven by the colorful cast of true Noranians who are also featured in Del Mundo's film.

Filipinos are famous for many things: our boxing skills, family values and universal talent for videoke. Yet one other thing that we can claim is our national obsession with stars. Between fame and fortune, Filipinos will choose fame, and this hypothesis is very much true in the life of Mandy Diaz -- the Superfan. If there's a saying that behind every great man is a great woman, then in the case of Ate Guy, she had a great gay.

Superfan also stars Teri Onor, Raisa Ver, and Mica Torre. Del Mundo's other credits include *Maid in Singapore*, *Ehemplo*, *Muni-muni*, and the best picture of the first Cinemalaya Independent Film Festival *Pepot Artista*. He is also the chairman of the Philippine Independent Filmmakers Multipurpose Cooperative.

Ooooo

ON STAGE

1. La Môme Celeste gives such lovely light

We are a musical race more than we are a literary, political or religious race. Already we have Nick Joaquin to light up our literary world, Manuel Quezon as the ultimate politician, and Lorenzo Ruiz as our saint. But where are our Mozart, our Rodgers & Hammerstein, our Edith Piaf?

Perhaps we already have.

It came like a tidal wave, the cheering audience rose in standing ovation for the girl on stage uncontrollably in tears. A man approached to hand her a kerchief and kiss her hand. And the tidal wave of Bravos! swept over the two, swirling and engulfing them for minutes.

We instinctively knew that a great moment has arrived. It is as if the trajectories of three lives -- one a composer from Pangasinan, the other the daughter of a great painter, and still another a jingle maker -- and the music of a whole nation -- had risen to their towering heights and met at precisely this point in time and place, CCP Main Theater, October 30, 1987.

The Great Filipino Song is yet to be born ... to catch the breath and inspire the heart and suffuse the mind like America the Beautiful by Katharine Lee Bates ... *O beautiful for spacious skies, for amber waves of grain,/ For purple mountain majesties above the fruited plain!/ America! America! God shed His grace on thee,/ And crown thy good with brotherhood from sea to shining sea!*

But we instinctively know that if it will ever be written... majestic and beautiful as our skies, seas and the winds that embrace us... the Great Filipino Song will emerge from the genius of the two people on that stage and perhaps one other.

That musical giant from Pangasinan Ryan Cayabyab will compose the music, that beautiful La Môme Celeste Legaspi will sing it to the world, and her husband that talented Nonoy Gallardo will write the lyrics.

Kuh Ledesma may dominate the stage with her elegance, Martin and Pops with the exuberance of their youth, and Nora Aunor with her sense of identity with the masses -- *ang galing, plakang plaka talaga kumanta!* -- but Celeste Legaspi stands head and shoulders above all as a true Filipino artist.

It takes more than talent and popularity to be a true artist. It takes commitment, love, generosity... above all, the ability to restate an eternal truth -- to distill the soul of a nation -- to crystallize the hopes, fears and aspirations of a people -- and bring forth the good, the beautiful and the common humanity of all men.

And that is what Celeste Legaspi has been doing all her life.

Like mathematical calculus, Celeste differentiates and integrates. Like Hegelian dialectics, she spirals in the logic of thesis, antithesis and synthesis.

In "*Pyano, Plawta, Saksopon at Bajo,*" Ernie M. Hizon recalls, Celeste sang *a capella* under the feline spell of a seductive saxophone... provided a naughty counterpoint to Cayabyab's unique arrangement of *Pipi* ... blithely described the traffic snarl and human sweat during the rush hours in *Limang Dipang Tao*... and musically interacted with the visual dimensions of Ed Castrillo's magnificent sculptures.

In "Celeste with Strings Attached," Celeste teased and taunted the gentle caresses of Demetillo's Spanish guitar... juxtaposed with the Chinese *pipa*, Japanese *samisen*, the Indian *sitar*, Indonesian gamelan... went through eight Salvador Bernal ternos in three minutes with a capsule history of the national dress as she sang *Dalagang Filipina*.

Then in "*Komiks Konsyerto*" and "*Sine, Sine*" Celeste invaded the twin towers of mass culture, comics and the cinema.

Filipino characters leaped out of the comic pages, as did *Mamaw* and Puff the Magic Dragon. Cayabyab's *Tsismis* and its alliteration (repetition), onomatopoeia (words that sound like their meaning), and nonsensical goobledegook merged with "jazzy syncopations and fevered scat singing."

In "*Sine, Sine*" like Czechoslovakia's masterful "Magic Lantern," Celeste blended cinema with life, singing a duet with Nora Aunor up on a giant screen; and with Ronnie Poe in a movie shoot-out, and villains Max Alvarado and Paquito Diaz onstage.

With her latest "Celeste, *Tunog* PPO" Celeste says goodbye to her series of "concept concerts," which started with "*Pyano, Plawta ...*" and now ends with a full sized Philharmonic Orchestra.

She will then move on to All-Filipino musical dramas, in search of the Great Filipino Song.

Critic Ernie M. Hizon: "In the concerts of Ms. Legaspi, the visual, aural and the Pinoy became one. Every presentation is a genuine *concertare*, a competition, a struggle, a battle between light and dark, joy and pain, earth and fire, sun and rain, mind and heart. Yet it is the Pinoy and his genius that always win out."

No space here to give justice to Celeste's last concert, but let us try.

On a bare stage the Philippine Philharmonic Orchestra sat -- ten First Violins, seven Second Violins, eight Violas, ten cellos, seven Bass violins, three Flutes and Piccolo, three Oboes and English Horn, three Clarinets and Bass-clarinet, three Bassoons and Contra-bassoon, six Horns, four Trumpets, four Trombones, one Tuba, four Tympani and Percussion, one Harp -- the greatest ever to play for a popular singer -- greater than the Big Bands of swing-and-sway, greater than Boston Pops -- in the background, veiled in gauze.

On center stage, Celeste sang *La Vie en Rose*, and *Hymne a L'Amour* -- through a mist of tears, we see a 14-year-old waif barely 5 feet tall, rising from the gutter to be the toast of Paris and of the world, singing songs of love through a life of drugs and despair, dying young of cancer and leaving our world bathed in the light of life and beauty.

La Môme Edith Piaf lives again in our own sparrow La Môme Celeste, with echoes of the sad refrain of every great artist:

I burn my candle at both ends,
I will not last the night,
But ah my foes and oh my friends --
It gives such lovely light!
November 5, 1987

2. What is wrong with showbiz in politics?

Movie Censor Manoling Morato wants not only to censor obscenity out of movies and TV, but also censor movie and TV stars out of the political scene. He objects to showbiz celebrities being elected to public office because of their immorality (are politicians any better?); their flights of film fantasy outside the hard realities of life; their topsy turvy schedules based on film shooting, off-beat fornication and night-clubbing; their lack of education (most being school drop-outs and drug addicts); their inability to speak good English or engage in debates; the inherent advantage of their pop popularity over others much more worthy of public service.

Manoling Morato who belongs to a political family -- his father Tomas was the first mayor of Quezon City, and has a main street named after him -- betrays the contempt of the *hifalutin* for the *hoipoloi*. Politicians have always been accepted into high society, actors usually are not.

Time was, centuries ago, when actors were considered wastrels and welchers, and actresses were considered women of loose virtue. Women were forbidden on the stage and women''s roles were once performed by transvestites. For a long time, it was an honored tradition on the Ateneo stage that women's roles were performed by the best looking boys.

Ed Olaguer, consultant of Jovy Salonga played Lady Macbeth. So did Danding Conjuangco's consultant JV Cruz. So did the late political whiz kid Rafael Hechanova. So did Senator Tito Guingona. "Screw your courage to the sticking place, and you will not fail!" Sounds obscene!

The late Lamberto Avellana and Sec. Raul Manglapus played Joan of Arc. Raul played Portia in "Merchant of Venice," and his consultant Edgardo "Hadji" Kalaw played Queen Elizabeth. Concert-goer Jose Lardizabal played hahaha the Player Queen in the play-within-the-play of "Hamlet."

Ex-Minister of Public Works Totoy Dans played the First Lord's sister in Gilbert and Sullivan's "H.M.S. Pinafore." The late La Salle president Waldo Perfecto played Viola and JV Cruz played Maria in "Twelfth Night." Actor villain Vic Diaz played Mrs. Malaprop. These he-men will never live it down, acting in drag.

People distinguish between stage and movie actors, saying that those on the stage are much more intelligent. They have to be, the stage is an actor's medium -- once the curtain rises, the actor is out of the control of the director and he acts out his role uninterrupted. The movie is a director's medium and the actors are his puppets, acting in non-sequential segments and often ignorant of what the director has in mind. The television is in-between, the director is still in control directing through floor directors, but the TV actors are no puppets.

Actors are often afflicted with a mammoth ego coupled with a monstrous sense of insecurity, their self-worth only as good as their last movie, play, concert or TV appearance. They are prone to bouts of high spirits and low depression, and are susceptible to the use of drugs, drinks and sex to achieve their highs. Their roles are often reflections of a permissive society, and they often to act out their movie roles in real life.

They live an exaggerated life in full view of the public, and the worst appear even worse than they really are. In the eyes of the public, Robin Padilla is nothing but a hoodlum, Martin Nievera is a loudmouthed brat; Alma Moreno, Zsa Zsa Padilla, Janice de Belen, Nadia Montenegro, Pilar Pilapil and all those fornicating brats on prime-time TV, are living beyond the pale of acceptable behavior.

Not all. There are artists we look up to -- the virginal Regine Velasquez, intellectual Eddie Garcia, do-gooder Rosa Rosal, religious Gary Valenciano, born-again Ray-An Fuentes, the late preacher Ronald Remy and his lovely daughter Jackie Kookooritchkin.

Like the rest of us, some artists are good in politics, some are no good. Erap Estrada is no idiot, he speaks good English, coming from a respectable family and educated in good schools, certainly better English than spoken by the Prime Minister of Japan or China leader Deng Xiaoping, and more understandable than Sen. Ernesto Herrera with his heavy Cebuano accent.

Erap is a committed Nationalist as is Nora Aunor, and as Vic Sotto is not. Sotto is a colonial idiot judging from his performance as front act for Cory's Bases Rally, with nothing more intellectual than a moronic "Yes to Bases!"

When the government needs to rally the citizens, it calls upon Dolphy and Ronnie Poe, not traditional politicians with no credibility. And all politicians have to sing and dance like actors to reach the masses.

Artists have an influence beyond their lifetime. And if they are anything like Erap and Nora, like Jane Fonda and Charlie Chaplin, singers like Sinatra and Bob Dylan, and writers like Shakespeare and Hemingway, they may say with pride:

"We are the music-makers,/ We are the dreamers of dreams,/ Wandering by lone sea-breakers,/ And sitting by desolate streams --/ Yet we are the movers and shakers/ Of the world and its people, it seems."
January 19, 1992

3. The divine spark of pure goodness

RJ Jacinto, stranger to me, introduced himself to me, a news columnist, and told me "a mere 3% of Filipino homes have newspapers, but 45% of the homes have TV sets and every home has at least 3 radio sets. I offer you the use of my radio and TV stations free of charge to widen your audience."   It was an astonishing act of generosity I will never forget. On June 3, 2015, RJ Jacinto celebrated his birthday with a concert of Rock and Roll music, with his friends Jose Mari Chan and Jim Paredes among others as guest performers.   Almost everyone I know were represented there. Tony Cojuangco, Jack Rodriguez, and Solar Sports' Wilson Tieng represented the Taipans and the business sector. Augustinian Father Horacio Rodriguez and several priests represented the religious sector.   There were politicians, government officials, lawyers, scientists, mathematicians, teachers, artists – my God, the assemblage was a microcosm of human society. All had a good time, and here among these people, I thought to myself, is "the divine spark of pure goodness" that is the best of every man.

I was sure this spark of divinity resides in the religious sector. No, I corrected myself. Millenniums before Christ, religion came in the form of a family of gods, mother-directed as all families are. Mothers are more tolerant, non-judgmental, and less obsessed with sex, and every man was privileged to adopt his own gods and bring them to a pantheon of gods that numbered as many as 2,000 in each culture. There was never any religious persecution; agriculture came into being, civilization flourished, and gave birth to the Greatness that was Egypt, that Glory that was Greece, and the Grandeur that was Rome. The Wonder that is China, under the influence of Teachers like Buddha and Confucius, and without religious intolerance, exists to this day. I imagine that when Jews came to Rome, and announced they were the Chosen People of the One True God, and consigned everyone else to hell, the Romans considered them a threat to public order, and said, "these Jews are a pain in the ass, let's throw them to the lions for entertainment. And while we're at it, let's do the same to Christians too. They are just as bad."

The advent and rise of the derivatives of Judaism – Christianity and Islam – also Father-directed, intolerant, vengeful, judgmental and bigoted -- led straight to the Dark Ages, with religious wars and persecutions that persist to this day, in Belfast between the Green Catholics and the Orange Protestants; in the Middle East between the Shi'ites and the Sunnis; in Mindanao between Muslims and Christians; and everywhere where Jews and Americans clash with Muslim jihads. There is no divine spark of pure goodness there. Catholicism owed its rise to power, to a fraudulent document called *Constitutum Constantini*, the Donation of Constantine, which gave temporal and spiritual power to the Catholic Church for 17 centuries of the 20 centuries, 85% of the Church's existence. The Donation was full of lies that spoke of cities that did not even exist at the time of Constantine. *E'craze l'infame*, destroy the infamous thing, exclaimed Voltaire!

I am a Catholic and an avid admirer of Pope Francis, but I do believe the most saintly Catholics are the female nuns like Mother Teresa, and that's because they are women who are by nature nurturers of the human race. But they are not the divine spark, rather a divine light, because they shine evenly and steadily, without spontaneity, explosive brilliance or uniqueness.

So where is this spark of divinity? Not among businessmen who are motivated by greed, responsible for the widening gap between rich and poor. Not among the scientists who created weapons of mass destruction. Maybe among mathematicians who explore the Mind of God, Absolute Truth in all its purity, harmony and balance, its greatest expression in equations like $E=mc^2$ which led straight to the nuclear bomb – oh hell, no divine spark among mathematicians either. Certainly not among politicians who are mostly corrupt, or among lawyers who are mostly liars. Maybe among the teachers, but that depends on what they teach.

How about the philosophers who do the thinking? – watch what you're thinking because Thoughts become Words; watch what you are saying because Words translate into Action; watch what you're doing, because Actions turn into Habits; watch your habits, because your Habits form your Character; and be aware of your character, because your Character will determine your Destiny. But destinies of great men may be evil too, like that of Hitler. No divine spark of pure goodness there either.

Now I come to the artists of this world – the painters, sculptors, poets, writers, and the music-makers, the dancers, singers, players, composers – very few of them are tainted with greed or selfishness or intolerance or bigotry – they have given all of us such joy and wonder, and they starve in attics; it is only when they die when we truly appreciate their work. In the field of music, specially, there is not a single trace of evil, not a single note of discord; in music there is a total absence of evil, and here then is the ultimate divine spark of pure goodness. No music ever caused physical harm or moral corruption. The divine spark is there in the soul of Jose Mari Chan and his sweet ballads; it is there in soul of Ramon Jacinto and his rock and roll. The two are forever smiling and singing, there is not a single mean bone in their bodies. If they have any flaws, it is only because they are born rich and because they are also businessmen. One can only speculate how much greater artists they would have been if they were as poor as Mozart.

I met Jose Mari Chan, sight unseen, when my daughter Elvira, then a high school student, came home with a wonderful tale of two youngsters who got married and came to Assumption Convent School to lay the bridal bouquet on the altar of the Chapel. One was Jose Mari, singing idol of the *collegialas*, and his new bride the beautiful Mary Ann – the sight gave Elvira a vision of perfect love that lasted her entire lifetime, and led her to collect Jose Mari's songs that filled our house with music. *WE are the music makers,/ And we are the dreamers of dreams,/ Wandering by lone sea-breakers/ And sitting by desolate streams --/ Yet we are the movers and shakers/ Of the world forever it seems.*

What makes America a great power is not its military might, it takes only cruelty and racism to be a big bully; nor is it its economic might, it takes only greed, obesity and wastefulness to take more than one's share of the world's scarce resources. What makes America great is what makes the world one global village: the pervasive presence of American music, movies, comics and junk food, and the English language as the *lingua franca* of the world. Of all these, it is American music that will last till to the end of time (like Europe's Mozart, Bach, Beethoven, now part of humanity's heritage). If the United States dominates the world, it is because, from the soul of the black slaves came the spirituals that spoke of human endurance, the minstrel songs that spoke of human hope and redemption, the funeral songs that spoke of deliverance, songs of Stephen Foster -- all that saw the birth of the jazz in New Orleans, evolving in the 20th century into the blues, boogie-woogie, soft and sweet, swing and sway, country and rock-and-roll -- American music that started to invade all cultures, inexorably, inevitably, despite all-out resistance from other countries. It is hard to imagine how the world would be today if Louie Armstrong, Ella Fitzgerald, Sinatra, Presley, and Streisand did not exist.

William Faulkner once wrote that "*Man is immortal simply because he will endure. When the last ding-dong of doom has clanged and faded from that worthless rock hanging tideless, in the last red and dying evening, even then there will still be one more sound: that of Man's puny inexhaustible voice still talking.*" Still singing too, and The Voice will be that of RJ or Jose Mari or Sinatra, an inexhaustible voice, "*because he has a soul, a spirit capable of compassion and sacrifice and endurance.*"
June 17-18, 2015

ooooo

BATMAN

1. Batman is a faggot, a fascist, a psycho?

The advent of the movie Batman Forever starring Vance Kilmer, as well as its two predecessors starring Michael Keaton, demands a series of comments. And our authority is my grandson Quark Henares.

In these days of Miranda doctrine, antiheroes and psychiatric analysis, for sometime now, human rights advocates, psychologists and intellectuals have been downgrading and demythizising our boyhood heroes. A Science Fiction writer Philip Jose Farmer wrote that Tarzan might have had sex with chimpanzees and eaten human flesh. James Bond is psychoanalyzed as having hatred and contempt for women. Jack of the Beanstalk is nothing but a thief. Superman is the personification of Might is Right, a fascist vigilante without respect for due process, a musclebound ape with no particular brilliance of mind. And so are Spiderman and Batman.

Worse than that, Batman (whose real name is Bruce Wayne) is a psycho, solely motivated by revenge for the murder of his parents by street thugs. Not only that, Batman may be a homosexual attached to his protégé Robin. Gays adopted him as their hero, and comedians refer to every closet queen as a Bruce. The charge that Batman is a faggot forced the producers of ``Batman, the movie" to take Robin out of the first two movies, although Robin was finally brought into the third film.

In vain was Bruce Wayne depicted by his fans as a playboy, with girlfriends like Julie Madison, Linda Page, Vicki Vale, even Batwoman, and the phantom female of ``The Demon of Gothos Mansion." To the end, Batman remained a bachelor, even though in the new film it is suggested that he got into bed with Nicole Kidman (in real life, girlfriend of Tomas Cruz, aka Tom Cruise)

Actually there were five Robins: Dick Grayson, an orphan of acrobats who was adopted by Bruce, and who finally left to join the Teen Titans because he needed to grow up; Jason Todd whose father was killed by Two Face, and who himself died in a violent explosion; Timothy Drake, the present Robin; Carrie Kelly, a girl (a reaction to the charge of homosexuality) and computer wizard, when Batman was an old man of 55 years; and Robert

Chang, after Bruce was long dead, when the grandson and namesake of Police Commissioner James Gordon decided to revive the "spirit of Batman." In the new movie, Robin is depicted as a combination of these -- an acrobat whose parents were killed by Two Face.

Batman was created by Bob Kane in the 1930s, and shared the comic page with Superman, Captain America, Green Hornet and the Phantom -- all of them heirs of literature's heroes with secret identities: Scarlet Pimpernel's Sir Percy Blakeney, Zorro's Don Diego Vega, The Red Shadow's Pierre Birabeau in the Sigmund Romberg operetta "The Desert Song."

Except for Al Capp's L'il Abner and Hal Foster's Prince Valiant, the comic strip (including Flash Gordon and Dick Tracy) remained by large a silly juvenile medium suitable only for children who stop reading the comics when adolescence and sex become a major distraction.

The first to graduate to an adult art form was Frank Miller's Batman.

2. Batman now an art form for adults

Batman was a two-dimensional comic strip hero for 50 years since he was created by Bob Kane in 1937. Then in 1986, Batman was transformed into a four-dimensional bundle of neuroses, by a new cartoonist, Frank Miller, in a book using computer-generated graphics. The book "The Dark Knight Returns" is a phenomenal development in the art of comics, a new approach to graphic story-telling that dealt with adult themes full of intensity, passion and power. It was a historic coming of age of a beloved art form.

In Miller's book, the Batman is portrayed as a middle-aged retired gentleman, as he re-emerges to recapture the spirit of his younger days. Here he fights and loses to a much younger foe, the leader of the teenage Mutants. Here he is accused of being a lawless vigilante, and attacked by SWAT teams sent to kill him.

Here Batman arranges the release of his old enemy Joker on humanitarian grounds, and later kills him in a gruesome and bloody battle. Here emerges the Sons of Batman, a organization of fanatic child vigilantes as murderous as the crooks they execute.

Here Superman joins Batman as a friend, who bungled in his attempt to protect the world from nuclear attack, and who was forced to engage in a gigantic battle to the death against the "lawless" Batman upon orders of higher authority.

Here the Batcave and all that is in it disappears forever, as it temporarily did in the movie "Batman Forever" under attack from Jim Carrey's Riddler. "The ancient moor trembles. Deep underground computers, holding every precious secret of the Batman, burst, and burn... Wayne's priceless collection of porcelain shatters, musically... empty stables fly apart like toothpick models... the central mass of Wayne Manor shudders, as if alive... then vanishes in a flash, bright as the sun. The world turns ruby red. The Manor roof rises, madly, into the sky, riding a pillar of flame."

Superman snarls to the crowd over the lifeless body of Batman, "Don't touch him!" In the graveyard, the priest commends his soul to God, and the TV newsgirl Lola Chong comments, "The spectacular career of Batman came to a tragic conclusion as the crime fighter suffered a heart attack while battling government troops. He has been identified as fifty-five year old Bruce Wayne... and his death has proven as mysterious as his life."

Here Gotham City which in Bob Kane's comic strip, once looked like Disneyland drawn in clear bright primary colors, becomes an unfriendly decaying inner city drawn in dark and sombre hues, just as depicted in the three Batman movies.

Indeed In his book, Frank Miller makes a true legend of Batman, with a depth of character and a fourth dimension -- time and old age taking its toll, and death -- like King Arthur's Excalibur sword flung into the lake, like Robin Hood's blind arrow to the site of his grave, like Davy Crockett in the Alamo. With Batman's final and greatest battle with Superman, Miller creates something spectacular and ultimate, something final and eternal, like Armageddon, the biblical end of the world, and Gotterdammerung, Wagner's twilight of the gods.

3. Batman from Year One to a century after Death

The story of Batman has been told many times by different authors in different ways: from Bob Kane's comic strip to the television hero played by Adam West mouthing outrageous camp dialogue, the radio version, two movie serials, two paperbacks, and a TV cartoon; and then the new graphic novels for adults, the latter a new art form of graphic story-telling, suffused with intensity and innovation. And now three adult movies produced by Tim Burton.

Frank Miller is not the only cartoonist aside from Bob Kane writing about Batman. There are Brian Augustyn (Gotham by Gaslight), Dennis O'Niel (Joker's Five-Way Revenge), Mike W. Barr (Batman: Year Two), Doug Moench (Last Story of Batman). Grant Morisson (Arkham Asylum), and Pepe Moreno (Batman: Digital Justice) -- writing about Batman from childhood to a century after death.

After chronicling the last years of Batman (The Dark Knight Returns), Frank Miller then explores Batman's beginnings (Batman: Year One) -- a story of urban violence and police corruption, painted in pastels, blacks and maroons.

Here we see a flashback of that night in Wayne Bruce's life, after seeing Tyrone Power in The Mark of Zorro with his parents -- when he watched them die in a dark alley by the hand of a frightened man with hollow eyes and a voice as brittle as glass -- and "all sense left my life." His twelve years abroad training as an athlete and scientist. His nightmares and that frightening night when a bat came crashing through the window of his study, "I shall become a bat." A shadow falls glisteningly wet, black against the black sky, and rises, a giant winged gargoyle, fading into the clouds -- Batman was born.

Here we see Selina, a whore with a collection of cats, become Catwoman, like Michelle Pfeiffer in the movie. Honest cop James Gordon triumphs over the crooks at City Hall, with a sordid love affair with other than his pregnant wife.

Grant Morisson wrote a psychological thriller, a terrifying journey into obsession and madness, "Arkham Asylum" (where the Riddler is confined in the movie). Here Joker and the rest of Batman's deformed and demented enemies, in padded cells and unlit cellars, rebel against the world of reason, and ask to have Batman come and mediate. In a harrowing contest of wits and wills with his greatest enemies, Batman descends into the heart of darkness, to confront his greatest fears and to realize that the madness of his enemies may be his own.

Pepe Moreno wrote "Batman: Digital Justice" with amazing computer-aided graphics made with latest Macintosh II -- with 3-D imaging, high resolution and direct-to-film printers, graphic scanners and a potential of 16 million colors. No physical drawings were made, only 200 megabytes of computer files.

Digital Justice tells the story by the end of the next century, long after Bruce Wayne and Batman had died, when every facet of man's existence is controlled by a vast computer network, invaded by a computer virus made by Joker a century before, with an agenda to dominate the world.

One lonely and angry policeman, James Gordon, the grandson of Batman's friend, with the resources of the entire civilization ranged against him, discovers the means to battle the Joker virus: the legend of Batman.

In all these stories, Batman has been dramatically redefined without contradicting any of his mythology in the hearts and minds of his comic fans. His story and those of his friends and enemies are consistently extrapolated, interpolated, elaborated on, psycho-analyzed, and reprised.

Batman manages to harmonize the varying facets of his character: a do-gooder, a vengeful psychopath, a fascist contemptuous of due process, a chimera right out of the darkest European fables, a legendary super-hero. Behind and beyond the imagery, themes and romance of the Dark Knight, lies a true classic of the myth and legend of Batman.

4. Batman Forever Bisexual

Batman Forever, the movie showing in the theaters nowadays is different from the first two starring Michael Keaton which are more subtle, more tongue-in-cheek, more sophisticated and more three-dimensional (with Keaton's acting) than this one starring Vance Kilmer who manages to endure the entire movie with a frozen face. Yet there is something in Batman Forever that weaves a spell even as it narrates, a riddle inside an enigma wrapped in a mystery. There is more than meets the eye. There is food for the psychiatrists, psychoanalysts and amateur head shrinkers, like my grandson Quark, so named because he is part of his father Atom. Quark looked at me as if I was a doddering dodo bird, and proceeded to give an analysis of the movie Batman Forever.

No, he is not talking about that nut James Carrey who will ever be an overgrown retardate with a face made of silicon putty, Quark said. Nor is he talking about Tommy Lee Jones, who plays Two-Face, a two-dimensional hood without credible motivation. No, we are talking about Batman and Robin, the Dynamic Duo. The movie confronts a question unanswered in the previous movies.   What is the true relationship between Batman and Robin?

Why is Robin called DICK, why does he insist on being Batman's "partner"? And why does Batman refuse with dread, as if to deny some feeling he might harbor, some horrible possibility that he doesn't dare confront, that he is after all a faggot, a gay, a homo, a queen. Why does he wear leather and rubber, as if he was into sado-machochism?

When pressured too much by Dick, he decides to quit being Batman and confused and frightened, he disappears from the public scene, as if to go back into his closet, afraid to come out and admit the truth.

When Dr. Chase Meridian (the gorgeous Nicole Kidman) indicated she wanted him in bed with her, he seems indifferent, or tortured by the thought he could not live up to her expectations. And when she finally told him she was in love with someone else, he felt relieved, his frozen face melted into a smile.

When the girl Chase is kidnapped by the villains, Dick offers his help to Batman who answers "A friend once taught me that a man should go his own way." Quark interprets this as Batman's way of saying that he wants to make his own decision whether he wants to be a homosexual or a heterosexual. Dick replies, "Not just a friend Batman, a partner," as if to say that Batman is being welcomed and accepted as a member of the gay community.

In the end Batman has to make a choice: whether to save Chase or Dick. According to Quark, at that moment Batman experienced what alcoholics refer to as the moment of clarity. And his decision is to save both, in effect saying. "To hell with the norm. This is the 1990's, the era of unisex and open-mindedness. I have made my decision, I am going to be both, I am going to be bisexual." After that, Batman rescued both Chase and Robin, and proceeded into forever.

The series of comic books telling and retelling the story of Batman, by different authors and in different ways, constitute a major break-through in the new art form of graphic story-telling. Supervised by DC Comics, and suffused with intensity and innovation, the story of Batman, from that of the television hero played by Adam West mouthing outrageously straight-faced camp dialogue; to comic strip features created by Bob Kane for the Sunday papers replete with Joker, Penguin, Tweedledum and

Rags and Riches

Tweedledee, Punch and Judy and Two Face, and additions to the Batman family, Batwoman, Batgirl, Bat Hound and Bat Mite; the radio version, two movie serials, two paperbacks, and a TV cartoon; and the new graphic novels for adults -- have been astonishingly consistent.

Batman whose every trivial and incidental detail is graven in stone on the hearts and minds of comic fans, has been dramatically redefined without contradicting any of his mythology. The roster of friends and villains are still there. But their stories are consistently extrapolated, interpolated, elaborated on, psycho-analyzed, and reprised.

Batman is still Bruce Wayne but he managed to blend and harmonize the varying facets of his character: a concerned do-gooder, a revenge-driven psychopath, a fascist vigilante contemptuous of due process, a ominous chimera right out of the darkest European fables, a legendary super-hero.

Behind and beyond the imagery, the themes and romance of the Dark Knight, lies a true classic of the myth and legend of Batman.

August 4-9, 1995, ISYU

ooooo

SHENANIGANS

1. Gethsemane of Alran, Seventh Heaven of Bobby and Jimmy

Minister Alran Bengson who might have been our new Executive Secretary has always been straight and true. Because of this, he is extremely sensitive about his reputation and insists on setting the record straight.

Alran was asked by the Palace to submit a plan for a transition period during which he will share power with and gradually take over from Joker. Alran was aware of the dangers of a transition that may take ten minutes or ten years, so he recommended that the President must make "an examination of conscience" and decide if she really wants Joker replaced, and if so, to do it right away with no transition period, because Alran cannot work with Joker.

That and a media blitz headlining the pending take-over of Alran as chief of staff, initiated by an assistant press secretary whose wife is the secretary of Alran, and by an editor known to be friendly to Alran, plus a subsequent press statement by Minister Ongpin timed to embarrass Joker --- all tended to give the impression that a campaign was being orchestrated to force the President into making a decision she was not yet prepared to make.

The subsequent uproar about the Council of Trent and the Octopus Diaboli bullying their way into a take-over, embarrassed Alran and agonized his frail and fragile wife. He frantically insisted on a "clarification" that he did not ask for the job, that it was offered to him, however vaguely.

It was this Gethsemane of Alran that made him and many others realize that he was not really cut out for the job of the Executive Secretary. He is too sensitive, too mindful of his integrity and reputation to discharge the one most important function of the Exec Sec, and that is to absorb all the pressures on the President, to take the blame for all the unpopular decisions.

So now, the President says she will keep Joker as her Exec Sec, and perhaps add to the office further. Alran will probably give way to the Council of Trent's back-up candidate --- the rightist-militarist, clerico-fascist Chito Ayala whose friends smell of death squads and the Spanish Inquisition. The plot thickens and sickens.

We read with delight, as we always do, Letty Magsanoc's piece on Flower Power, about her friend Bobby Borja who discovered the aesthetics of growing bougainville vines on Meralco's power lines. Our reaction to this inspired act is to advise Bobby to pay up on all back insurance premiums, triple the insurance coverage, subscribe to funereal services of the most expensive type, go to confession and communion, kiss the folks goodbye -- and invite Jimmy Ongpin to stand with him beside his bougainville vine during a thunderstorm.

We assure him that sooner or later, when charged electrons with sufficient electromotive force, accept the invitation to rush down the wet vine, now fully transformed into an efficient electrical conductor, Bobby Borja and Jimmy Ongpin will find themselves in Seventh Heaven. Bobby will be spared all the expenses of incineration and cremation, leaving his heirs with more than enough resources to plant bougainvilleas on his grave, and his rich widow with enough attraction to acquire more husbands willing to take out insurance and continue the lucrative pursuit of Flower Power. With Jimmy Ongpin gone, perhaps we can improve our economy and pay our debts.

Talking about Jimmy Ongpin and our burgeoning external debt, we mentioned before that the loan notes signed by governments in debt are being bought and sold among financial institutions. The latest quotations indicate that Peru's loan notes are discounted 80 percent and are being sold at 20 percent of face value. Our own loan notes are discounted only 28 percent, and are being sold at 72 percent of face value.

Of course nations in debt are legally forbidden to buy back their loan notes, because that would constitute "prepayment" over which other conditions are imposed. But Peru has contracted secret agents to buy back these loan notes at a substantial discount, thus paying back the loan at 20 cents to the dollar. This is an open secret Peru and its creditors would never publicly confirm, for obvious reasons.

And to get its citizens in on a good deal, Peru is asking its citizens to buy these discounted notes, and use the notes to pay for Peruvian goods for export, crediting them with a good part of the full value of the notes in local currency.

Applied here in the Philippines, it means that a buyer may purchase a discounted note with face value of $500, paying only $100 for it; then using this note to pay for $300 worth of coconut oil, and exporting this coconut oil for $300 with a clear profit of $200, while the country gains $200 on the deal, paying back an obligation of $500 with only $300 worth of goods. This encourages massive exportation of coconut oil, and rapid repayment of our loans.

Peru keeps the loans at 20 percent of face value by limiting its debt service payments to 10 percent of export proceeds, and by judicious release of bad news. This way, Peru has achieved a phenomenal growth of more than 10 percent this year, compared to our almost zero growth.

By constantly reassuring the debtor banks of our willingness to pay in full regardless of the state of our economy, Jimmy Ongpin has kept Philippine loans at a comparatively higher price of 72 percent of the face value. Jimmy Ongpin should have his salary paid by the IMF and the American banks, he works for their side of the fence.

Someday, Jimmy Ongpin, the Council of Trent and the Octopus Diaboli will take over Malacañang, and when they do, our loan notes will be worth 100 percent of the face value in the open market.

Someday, Jimmy will get his reward as a consultant of the World Bank, like Cesar Virata, at $500 a day. That's more than P10,000 a day, more in one day than a poor Filipino schoolteacher earns in a year. Dung.

March 24, 1987

2. Is Alran the power behind Cory's throne?

When Health Secretary Alran Bengson decided that he wanted to take the Population Control Commission from the supervision of the Department of Social Welfare and Development, Sec. Mita Pardo de Tavera complained to Exec. Sec. Joker Arroyo that more than a third of her budget would be lost.

But Alran argued that Population Control is more than merely a question of social development. Its ultimate purpose is reduce population pressure on economic development, so that increases in Gross National Product are not negated by increases in population growth. The Population Control Commission should therefore be under NEDA Sec. Solita Monsod.

Undaunted Mita Pardo de Tavera brought three Bishops to Malacañang to argue her case, which is really to make sure that the Church policy on birth control be strictly followed, with a snide remark that Solita's family were originally non-Catholic.

Mita won the battle, but not the war.

By getting the two women to do the fighting, Alran was in effect preparing himself as the compromise choice. Solita quarreled with the Council of Trent over the debt negotiations. The Council cut down the powers of her office with the consent of Cory; Solita got the message and resigned.

From all over the world, especially the United Nations and the USA, came advice that following the Opus Dei and the conservative elements of Church in their opposition to Population Control is irreparably disastrous to any economic development.

The big joke among the Americans is that the Pope has neither qualifications nor moral authority to impose his opinions on how we act inside the bedroom, "You no play da game, so why you make da rules, eh?"

Opus Dei George Winternitz goes around telling us that the dwindling population in developed nations result in having more old people being supported by fewer of the young.

Like the Opus Dei argument that excess of nationalism leads to imperialism -- when applied to poor nations with no job opportunities and without a sense of nationhood, it is tantamount to lecturing a starving man on the evils of over-eating.

Finally the Population Commission was entrusted to the Health Department and to Alran Bengson. And the USAID budgeted $40 million dollars for this program over five years.

This is the reason Congressmen Leonardo Guerrero, Ronnie Zamora, Nani Perez and others associated with Speaker Mitra strongly suspect Alran Bengson who once called Mitra a liar, as the chief architect of the Kabisig Movement.

According to their reasoning, with $40 million or P8 billion by their calculations, actually P880 million, programmed for population control, Alran will have the facilities to mobilize doctors, midwives and rural workers, and send them into every home in the country, to organize mothers, fathers, teachers, even priests and nuns into a socio-political movement.

What is going on? What is the agenda of my cousin Alran? The Ateneo Survey of Father Kinik Bernas, Rasputin of the Council of Trent, shows that the first three in the popularity poll in descending order, are Fidel Ramos, Oscar Orbos and Alran Bengson -- all from Pangasinan, aha!

Defense Secretary Fidel Ramos finds his Army divided and no room for him in political parties, what else is he going to do? Join the Kabisig, of course.

Oscar Orbos, fair-haired boy of both Mitra and the President is a prisoner of his job as DOTC Secretary, and is expected to join the Kabisig as a deodorizer -- practically the only one left in the Cabinet with high credibility, and perhaps destined to preside over the death of political parties.

Alran Bengson who is the recipient of P880 million from the USAID, plus the obligatory counterpart funds from our own government -- is also the vice-chairman of the Bases Negotiating Panel!

This is what drives Congressmen up the wall -- the very thought that not only Big Business of the Makati Business Club, the Church of Cardinal Sin, Opus Dei of Jess Estanislao and the Army of Fidel Ramos are behind the Kabisig, but also the Almighty Uncle Sam of Kulas Platypus.

Here they are, willing to sell out to the Americans on the bases -- and they are being left out of the pay-off. Why, it is enough to drive these colonial morons to nationalism, heaven forbid.

Reminded that the same church choir boys in the person of Soc Rodrigo, Manuel Manahan and Raul Manglapus never made it without a political party, Congressmen say: "This is different. Alran does not need a party, he has the President, Uncle Sam, the Church, Big Business, and the Army as well. And he works from within, not from without."

Alran Bengson -- future President? Kingmaker? power behind the throne? flunky for Cesar Buenaventura? or a master strategist for a re-election president?

July 11, 1990

3. Alran is anomaly in Council of Trent

HEALTH Secretary Alran Bengzon is an original, full-fledged and second most influential (first is Shell's Cesar Buenaventura) of the Council of Trent, real masters of our destiny.

His brother in the ConCom was one of the Four Horsemen of Dick Holmes, CIA agent who masterminded loopholes in the Constitution that preserved the American bases, American monopoly, and our plantation type of colonial economy.

He was the best friend of Jaime Ongpin, and was hand-picked by him as the new Executive Secretary in the aborted attempt by the Council to evict Joker Arroyo. He is the leading light in the effort to perpetuate his Ongpin's memory, in an their alma mater Ateneo University and in a book commissioned from National Artist Nick Joaquin.

Yet he is a Nationalist, and in a way he stands for everything the Council of Trent is against: Faith in the Filipino, and unqualified loyalty to our nation without the colonial double-allegiance of pro-American surrogates.

For he did what the Council of Trent would consider anti-American, and therefore subversive.

First, all by himself he was able to impose the Generics Act on the multinational drug corporations for the sake of the Filipino people, in spite of a multi-million dollar lobby by the Drug Association with all the help of the Makati Business Club, American Chamber, American Embassy and every visiting VIP from Washington DC. This alone should make Alran anathema in the eyes of American neanderthals of low IQ and their surrogates in the Council of Trent.

Then, in Dong Puno's television show, Alran Bengzon as the government's Peace Commissioner, chided the Armed Forces, saying, "I do not think the Operation Thunderbolt in Negros Occidental is worth the social cost."

Alran was referring to the AFP's all-out offensive and forced evacuation of 35,000 civilians from their lands -- what many critics call the Vietnamization of my poor province. This is enough to mark Alran for assassination by CIA death squads determined to plunge our nation into a civil war under their LIC bloodbath policy.

What makes the man tick? How was he able to sponsor the Generics Act and chide the army without being drummed out of the Council Trent as a pro-Filipino bastard? Why do the neanderthals tolerate such sacrilege -- for which so many of our labor leaders, students, priests and intellectuals have already been tortured and murdered by CIA death squads?

First, because Alran Bengzon is not confrontational. He does not provoke like most nationalists do. He waits for his idea to mature, to be accepted by the powers-that-be and the people, and then he acts.

We nationalists like to think that we accelerate this movement along the same lines and in the same direction. We have our own role to play in the scheme of things. We initiate, we raise the flag of combat, we provoke, we drive the idea along, we push it... till at last we hand it over to a guy like Alran who has the patience and persuasive powers to bring it to fruition.

I suppose if the Civil Rights movement has Abraham Lincoln and Martin Luther King, so did the Nationalist Movement here have Jose Rizal and Claro M. Recto. And if the Civil Rights has Earl Warren of the US Supreme Court to make it a final reality, so does the Nationalist Movement have Tañada, Diokno and in a small way Alran Bengzon to give it a final push.

Twenty years ago I attempted without success to promote Generics as a solution to American monopoly and high drug prices. I failed miserably, the drug lobby were running rings around me and the Congress.

Only last year Alran Bengzon of the Council of Trent accomplished what I failed to do. He made me feel that ideas have a time frame of their own, with a quote from Victor Hugo: "Mightier than the march of armies is an idea whose hour has come."

Second is that he is a team player who is most influential with President Cory who respects his humble and wise counsel. The Council of Trent needs him more than he needs the Council. In departments outside his own responsibility, Alran Bengzon cooperates in projects dear to the heart of the neanderthals -- like the acceptance of IMF conditionalities and the American bases. Apparently he feels as a nationalist that the time is not ripe to challenge these abominations.

Alran Bengzon is a gentle person averse to front page publicity and public confrontations, and is sensitive to the feelings of others. It is precisely because of these admirable qualities that he lost out in the Council's bid to have him appointed as Executive Secretary.

It is a possibility to speculate on -- what will a nationalist like Alran do when confronted by the pro-American Council of Trent?

July 24, 1989

4. House at P1,800/mo., earn P15,000/mo.

Mr. George Marcelo, an old friend and *compadre* of mine and son of Jose P. Marcelo who helped finance political campaigns of Macapagal and Marcos, has emerged after 35 years to present a proposition for mass housing that will cost the government nothing, the $500 million investment to be financed by the Sultan of Bahrain, with absolutely no need for any government guarantee. His project will provide 10,008 houses at a rental of P1,800 a month for 35 years, after which the ownership will be transferred to the occupant. George Marcelo's project is much more than a housing program, it is also an industrial project that will provide employment for 20,000 people at P15,000 a month, and will earn an export income of US$166 million per year. He expects to accomplish this in 18 months after the necessary government approvals from PEZA for tax-exemption and DENR for environment clearance.

He does this by setting up an Industrial and Aqua Farming Park that is globally competitive even against the competition of China. Building houses and a factory on expensive land is out of the question, so George will build them on the sea, in Cavite's Bacoor Bay, right near the airport. The houses will be in hexagonal modules of styropor encased in glass fiber and polyeurethane, the same used in the Marcelo boats made for the Navy, interconnected with pontoon walkways. The entire complex including the min-factories, is designed with hexagonal modules by the Architect Hans Bohlmann and Brown & Root engineers of Australia, guaranteed to withstand 250 kilometer/hour winds (40% stronger than required by the local code).

Imagine, the houses contain a living space of 25 square meters per module, all fully furnished with furniture, kitchen appliances, sofa beds, light fixtures, even cutlery, plates and utensils. Each house will have free electricity generated by Solar Cells. And free potable water desalinized by reverse osmosis from the sea. There are cement pilings that keep the buildings from swaying and moving sideways to keep one from getting sea-sick. The houses will be occupied by his workers in the factory, paying only P1,800 per month for rent and being paid P15,000 per month for their labor. Not bad deal at all.

George's project will not use Meralco power but will instead generate its own, (1) with solar cells getting electricity from the sun; (2) a Solar heat panels and a natural gas burner that will supply high pressure steam to a turbine generator; (3) Wind Power Turbines to supplement Solar Power; (4) Fuel Cells generating electricity with the use of hydrogen liberated from water by electrolysis.

Neither will George's project use water from the Nawasa. As part of the process to produce salt, the project will produce 120,000 cubic meters of water every day, 85,000 of which will be sold to Nawasa/Maynila. By Reverse Osmosis, the seawater is desalinized, producing potable water and 1.5 million metric tons of commercial salt which is exported to Japan and Korea. But most of the industrial salt (priced only $30 per ton) will be processed into Chlorox bleaching agent (liquid and flakes) and exported at $2,000 per ton.

There is a working model of the housing in Marcelo Steel Corporation Compound in Punta, Sta. Ana, Manila, and a working model of pontoon walkways at the Manila Yacht Club. The export market guaranteed by Itochu and Marubeni, the largest Japanese trading companies in the world.

He already has the approval of the City of Cavite, National Housing Authority, but is having trouble with PEZA (Undersecretary Ortaliz and someone in Malacañang whom he will identify if asked) and DENR (whose consultants quote P2 million to make their own study, which no other country even charges). George claims that there is already a study by Brown & Root which shows a zero-waste, environment friendly system.

This project uses cutting edge technology successful in small scale to create an industry of global competitiveness. A ray of hope for the Philippines.

September, 2001

5. Mess at the FTI: Jaime de la Rosa is in hot water

THIS week Jaime de la Rosa may be fired from his job. He has a brother whose name is Rogelio de la Rosa, but he is not the movie star.

He is the president and general manager of the Food Terminal Inc. (FTI), and like his predecessor Emil Ong, he is being accused of anomalies and indiscretions.

Before the Ombudsman he is accused of collecting double compensation contrary to law, receiving the salaries and allowances of both president and general manager; also of using a government vehicle on a Sunday celebration of his birthday, which vehicle, driven by his unlicensed daughter, was involved in an accident that cost the FTI P57,000.

Before a probe body organized by his boss National Food Administrator (NFA) Pelayo Gabaldon, he is accused of the same plus having contrived an anomalous contract with an unqualified security agency, and having committed acts of lasciviousness unbecoming a government official.

In view of press statements giving piecemeal information and the pending resolution of de la Rosa's case by his superiors this week, we present this two-part series based on an interview with de la Rosa, to clarify the issues, because these issues affect so many other government officials.

Mr. de la Rosa was FTI general manager when he was appointed president as well, upon the recommendation of the previous president, Atty. Maria Asuncion Rodriguez Tinga, wife of Congressman Dante Tinga of Taguig-Pateros. The FTI is a fully owned subsidiary of National Food Administration.

On March 1, 1990, he assumed the two posts and received the salary and allowances of both positions, amounting to P35,735 per month (as general manager he received P19,000).

He did so on the authority of a June 1990 resolution by the FTI Executive Committee, giving him ``the allowances due the President of FTI,'' effective retroactively from March 1990. To his accusers, this is a clear violation of Section 8, Article IX(B) of the Constitution prohibiting double compensation for public officials, unless specified by law.

De la Rosa claims that he receives only the ``honorarium'' of the president who had no salary, and such honorarium was collected by Emil Ong in addition to his salary as NFA administrator (he could not have done so today after a Supreme Court decision disallowing multiple positions by officials).

But the president does not occupy an honorary position, he is chief excutive officer. The ``honorarium'' (about P20,000) was his only compensation, considered the salary of his predecessor Atty. Tinga. Salary vouchers show that de la Rosa gets a basic monthly salary of P10,655 and representation allowance of P25,080 a month, of which, he claims, only about P16,000 represents extra compensation from his position as president.

Unless the two positions were merged and a new compensation scale is given, de la Rosa as a public official has violated the Constitution. But de la Rosa claims that in a labor dispute, the Supreme Court ruled that the FTI is not a government corporation under the GSIS, but a private corporation under the SSS. Therefore, he says he is not a government official as defined in the Constitution.

That is not correct, all that was settled was that FTI employees are not in the Civil Service, like all elective officials, the PNB and the Central Bank. But any one paid out of public funds is a government employee, and is subject to constitutional prohibition against double compensation.

Jaime de la Rosa is also accused of using an FTI vehicle for non-official purposes, falsification of public documents and malversation. On Sunday, May 13, 1990, de la Rosa admitted using an FTI Hi-Ace van (official trip ticket no. 902109) for his birthday party in Napindan, Taguig. On the way back to Ayala Alabang, the van sideswiped two pedestrians, Jennifer Napao and Leonora Salamanca. The victims were hospitalised at the cost of P57,000, of which P18,000 was paid by insurance and P39,000 paid by the FTI.

His accusers say that Jaime's 18 year-old daughter Jinky who has no driver's licence, was at the wheel, but official documents made it appear that the FTI driver Edgardo Navarro was driving the van.

Eyewitnesses Joel Fernandez and Luzviminda Manzanilla attested to this, while de la Rosa questions why they executed their affidavits June 1991, one year after the accident occurred. This is irrelevant. Victim Leonora Salamanca affirmed the allegation. A cover-up was necessary to absolve the poor girl of guilt and to collect on the insurance.

These two issues, on collection of double compensation, and on those arising from his birthday bash, have been elevated to the Ombudsman for prosecution under the anti-graft law. But three other issues are raised before a probe committee formed by NFA administrator Pelayo Gabaldon and Agriculture Sec. Senen Bacani.

IT is unconstitutional for a government official to accept emoluments of more than one position, no matter how many positions he holds. He should not appropriate government vehicles for his personal use or that of his family, specially on Sunday; or allow his child to drive it, specially when she does not have a driver's license, or get the driver to take the blame if she gets into an accident.

Also a government official should not travel abroad on a trip financed by someone he does business with, or hug and kiss his women employees maliciously or when drunk, or favor a bidder against the advice of the bidding committee. If his accusers are to be believed, that's what FTI president and general manager Jaime de la Rosa did. And he may be fired this week if the accusations prove to be true.

In addition to what he was accused of before the Ombudsman, of receiving double compensation, of using public vehicles for non-official purposes, falsification of public documents, and malversation of public funds, Jaime de la Rosa is accused of lascivious acts unworthy of an official.

Three photographs show Jaime de la Rosa taking liberties with a recently widowed woman employee during a Christmas party in the Utilities and Transportation department of the FTI last December 1990. Asked to explain, he said he could not even remember the incident. His accusers say he was either drunk, or he does this so often that he forgets with whom he did it. Among us boys, the practice seem harmless and katuaan lang, but in these days of videocams, instamatics, born-again self-righteousness, and a religious President Cory, it is fatal, specially for public officials.

Jaime de la Rosa is also accused of favoring a bidder People's Security despite the negative findings of the Bidding Committee and the ``Corplan'' against People's, and over the objections of the Chairman of the Bidding Committee, Deputy General Manager Donato Estacio.

De la Rosa argues that the committee itself, including Estacio, recommended People's Security by giving it the highest rating among the six agencies being considered. However, close look at the committee report shows that ``Corplan'' considered People's from past experience as ``not solvent and liquid and unable to meet current obligations,'' and supervisors point out its inadequacies in firearms, vehicles and communications equipment, according to Estacio.

The conclusions of two committee members have all the earmarks of a railroad. They added two other criteria (in usual practice the criteria is set long before the bidding is done). After giving People's the lowest score on net worth, on a new criteria of ``Agency Highlights'' they rated every bidder zero except People's and Lockheed, to which they gave a maximum 10 percent each.

With this one scandalously dubious step, People's and Lockheed were catapulted from cellar position to first and second place, respectively. Talagang lutong makaw. And this was accepted by de la Rosa.

Lastly FTI head Jaime de la Rosa is being accused of being too chummy with a Danny Arrieta, a lessee who has not paid his rental for the last 18 months, amounting to some P1.6 million, and who ``accompanied'' de la Rosa and his wife for a 5-day pleasure trip to Tokyo April or May 1991.

Not true, said de la Rosa, ``My wife Anita and I traveled in the company of Taguig Mayor Rodolfo de Guzman and his wife Carmen.'' Not the whole truth, said his accusers, Danny Arrieta went ahead through Seoul and met them in Tokyo.

Tokyo is the most expensive place in the world, with hotel coffee selling at $10 (or P300) a cup. All tourists avoid Japan, what was de la Rosa doing there, a place he cannot afford except as a guest of someone?

We asked de la Rosa, why all these woes are being showered on him at the same time? His accusers are Benjamin Juta and Ed Gacusan, former FTI employees. But de la Rosa accuses Deputy General Manager Donato Estacio and Congressman Dante Tinga for being behind all these plots against him.

He says that Donato Estacio, whom he relieved of all functions for objecting to the award to People's Security and who in turn feels like a marked man, is aspiring to take the his place as president and general manager if he is fired or made to resign.

Congressman Tinga, according to de la Rosa, has political reasons for getting him out, his brother Rogelio de la Rosa being Capitan del Barrio and president of the Association of Barangay Captains (ABC) from which he was forced to resign, and Jaime de la Rosa himself being bruited about as a candidate for congressman. De la Rosa denied any political ambitions.

Ridiculous, Tinga who bested Enrile's sidekick Rene Cayetano and is a big man inside Congress, need not fear any threat from the de la Rosa brothers, even if they have the same names as movie stars.

August 13, 15, 1991

6. Awards to 20 'solons' hahaha

I really do not know what I am doing here as guest speaker of Congress Magazine and the Makati School of Journalism and Arts, which are giving awards to 20 congressmen.

Firstly. I have been invited by its president and my good friend Frankie Grego, whom I knew from the good old days of Recto and the National Crusade, and it is hard to say no, because there are so few of us Rectonians left.

Nationalists have long been considered Communists by the CIA, and with the end of the Cold War, are now officially declared extinct by the IMF, World Bank, GATT, WTO, and the APEC. On the 100th anniversary of the 1898 Revolution, we find Rizal, Bonifacio and Aguinaldo no longer relevant. Here in the birthplace of Asian Nationalism, we Filipinos no longer consider ourselves as Filipino citizens. We are now Citizens of the World.

Secondly, I warned Frankie Grego not to confuse his guests with wrong directions. Hotel Shangri-La is in Makati; Shangri-La Edsa Plaza simply does not exist except as plain Edsa Plaza. How green is my valley, simply known as Greenbelt located in Makati where civilization exists. On the other hand, Greenhills is in "them thar hills" known as Ortigas, where Japanese stragglers are probably still holding out. Valleys are not hills or mountains. Never shall the twain of Greenbelt and Greenhills meet in the confused minds of ordinary mortals.

The Pasig River is the border between civilization and barbarism, and further out where Congress meets, Quezon City is simply a city of Vandals where street signs are regularly missing and house numbers are not in sequence, going up and then coming down and then running sideways, because QC people are loath to change the addresses on their old letterheads, and house signs. That is the reason I got lost on my way here, sorry.

Third, how come I find myself addressing a group of congressmen who, as politicians, do most of the talking and none of them listening? I am even surprised that they are here at all. In Congress they rarely, if ever, are present in enough numbers to constitute a quorum.

Fourth, I am even more surprised to note that among the members of Congress, there is an Edcel Lagman for every Junior de Guzman, and a Joker Arroyo for every Romy Jalosjos -- although there are not enough of the good ones to censure the bad ones.

Fifth, I am not only surprised but profoundly astounded to be informed by Frankie Grego that in the unexpressed thoughts of Ninez Cacho Olivares "among the clowns and morons, crooks and traitors, there at least 20 congressmen who are truly worthy of emulation and recognition." Correction please, I can count only 10. I only wish Ninez Cacho Olivares were here to share with us this truly significant occasion, akin to the Red Sea Crossing and the birth of Christ.

Making a speech on such occasion should be something like delivering the Sermon on the Mount or the Gettysburg Address, short and sweet and to the point.

So, after these preliminary remarks, I shall now delivery my main address. My address is Dasmariñas Village, Makati. I thank you.

February 20, 1997, ISYU.

7. Tet wins his lonely battle

Remember that movie *Back to Bataan* made way back in 1945, starring John Wayne and Anthony Quinn? It is the story of the Fall of Bataan, the Death March and the comeback of our guerillas against the Japanese occupation forces. A stupid ignorant scriptwriter made Anthony Quinn play the part of Andres Bonifacio Jr., son of our hero who actually never sired a child.

But *Back to Bataan* was a well-made, exciting war drama about a heroic struggle of John Wayne against all odds in the face of superior force.

Today we see a remake in the epic struggle of Rep. Tet Garcia against foreigners and the palace cronies who sought to transfer the petrochemical project from Bataan to Batangas, after the BOI granted the Taiwanese investors tax exemptions, massive financing through the ADB and the PNB, and dollar gifts through CB re-lending scheme and debt-equity swaps.

The Supreme Court after three adverse rulings, finally supported Tet's petition to annul the BOI approval allowing the Taiwanese to move the plant to Batangas. *Back to Bataan* is an appropriate title for this lonely and triumphant fight of Tet against all odds, truly a feat worthy of John Wayne.

I remember more than a year ago when Enrique Garcia asked me for an appointment. I had an eerie feeling of *deja vu* as I recalled Health Secretary Enrique Garcia with wife Fanny showing up at my house at six in the morning, saying, "I came to say goodbye, Larry, I am dying of cancer."

"I am Rep. Tet Garcia from Bataan," the voice said, "And I have something that is in line with your recent Meralco exposè."

At lunch he gave me a voluminous folder on the "conspiracy" of the Board of Investment, Filipinas Shell, and the Taiwanese investors to transfer the projected petrochemical plant from its original site in Bataan to Batangas. I told him it is a hopeless fight.

In a way, I was right. Three times the Supreme Court ruled in favor of BOI. But Tet persisted.

Months later, he told me that Malacañang itself, under the influence of a top Shell official, offered him pork barrel funds and other industrial projects if he withdrew his objection to the plant transfer.

He filed a new petition before the Supreme Court, and is facing formidable opposition from Sycip-Salazar representing the Taiwanese and Romulo-Mabanta representing Shell, law firms that "never" lose cases in the Supreme Court; from CB Gov. Jobo Fernandez, Finance Sec. Ting Jayme, DTI Sec. Joe the Immaculate Misconception and BOI vice Chairman Tammy Alcantara; from columnists Max Soliven (Star), Rodolfo Romero (Bulletin) and others.

He begged "Help! I am alone and I need an Equalizer." How could I refuse? To be a Horatio at the bridge, to be the Voice in the Wilderness, to be alone in a black pit from pole to pole, bloody but unbowed -- this is the stuff of which Tet Garcia and heroes are made. Practically alone among the journalists, I helped him.

I looked into Shell Company for whose benefit the transfer was being made. I wrote about the "white elephant" $100 million Shell LPG entrepôt in Tabangao, Batangas, and its failure to entice LPG customers in Thailand, Malaysia and Brunei.

I wrote about Shell's hope to have the petrochem plant use as feedstock, the LPG imported by Shell instead of the naphtha produced by Petron in Bataan.

I wrote about Shell's LPG tank farm in Biñan, set up there over the objections of its mayor and residents (including Ombudsman Conrado Vasquez) who fear being incinerated by hellish fire.

I wrote about the original BOI decision to place the plant near its naphtha source, Petron of Bataan; the comparative safety of gas emissions in mountainous and non-populated area (as against the populated Batangas site); the grant of 576 hectares of free public land for the plant and its downstream industries (as against speculative land ventures in Batangas).

Then one night in Casino Español, Joker Arroyo told me he will expose the next day the Petroscam, whose capital was to come mostly from behest loans, the ADB allocation for Philippine projects, and dollar gifts through CB relending and debt-equity schemes. Tet Garcia threatened to resign his congressional seat if justice is not served.

The Supreme Court first ruled that due to the incentives given by the government and the nationalistic provisions of the Constitution, the government (BOI) must finally decide on the plant site on the basis of national interest alone.

Then the Supreme Court now ruled that the BOI cannot give the Taiwanese investors complete authority to choose the site, since the BOI originally chose Bataan as the ideal site for valid economic and technical reasons.

President Cory Aquino publicly stated that she will abide by the decision of the Supreme Court, while Joe the Immaculate Misconcepcion and Tammy Alcantara, unmindful of the fact that the Senate wants them censured for undue interest in the Petroscam, howled their intention to seek reconsideration of the Supreme Court decision. Sad, sad.

Back to Bataan, so much like John Wayne, is a tribute to lonely splendor of Tet Garcia's battle against all odds, and to the Supreme Court proving once again that against wealth and power, justice still prevails!

November 23, 1990

8. Pests and Pirates

Many people in the National Telecommunications Commission (NTC) which I used to frequent to get my radio amateur's license, told me confidentially that some mayor in Batangas wrote a sizzling insulting letter complaining about me. I am not particularly an admirer of mayors in the sticks and the boondocks, so I decided to investigate.

I found out he is a Tito Toledo, President and Chairman of Katigbak Enterprises who complains that a "Mr. Henares" is guilty of "a blatant lie and disinformation" and is heading a media blitz in Metro Manila to discredit his small FM station DZWI-FM (Power

108, on 107.9 MHz, with a station 200 meters from Tagaytay for interference in Metro Manila area. I regret everybody assumes it is myself he is referring to, when it is obviously my son Atom who owns the NU-107 on 107.5 MHz which suffer from the interference.

You should know what kind of a person this Mayor Toto Ojeda is. Sometime ago he bought or leased a station in Manila, never operated it, and never paid for it. He was sued by the original owner. Eventually the NTC authority lapsed, and NTC took back the frequency. This time Tito Ojeda used the frequency without authority, was sued by the NTC, and eventually he pulled out. That is the kind of operator this man is. He is now operating a Batangas FM station station at least 200 meters near Tagaytay City spilling a big portion of his signal into Metro Manila so near to the frequency of Atom's NU-107.

There are only a few FM stations that can be accommodated in the prime market of Metro-Manila, some 23 or 24 stations between 88 to 108 MHz, each separated from its neighbor at the dial by a strict international standard of 80 kilohertz or 0.8 MHz. That is why each station is 0.8 MHz apart. 104.3 my Business Radio, 105.1, 105.9, 106.7, 107.5 Atom's station -- all separated by 800 kilohertz. Yet only 400 kilohertz away, on 107.9 is this Tito Ojeda's station, clearly heard in Manila because it is deliberately located in the mountains near Tagaytay. The KBP protested and the NTC ordered Ojeda to move the station elsewhere or stop using the 4-Bay Jampro Circular Polarization Antenna that also sends signals directly opposite to its service areas in the Calabarzon region.

This is not the first time a pest and a pirate of the airwaves tried to intrude upon the Manila area. Five years ago Benny Rebuano, also from Batangas applied for the same frequency 107.9 MHz, to be placed in Tagaytay. A hearing was conducted and his application was DENIED. Now Tito Ojeda wants the same, claiming to be a politician of NUCD, and brazenly dropping the name of Secretary Renato de Villa whom I personally know to be a boy scout at heart and won't be caught dead helping Ojeda in a caper like this. Also he's been dropping the name of congressmen Raffy Nantes and Congresswoman Lyn Punzalan who should know their names are being used to justify an unlawful act.

But as long as Tito Ojeda's station is heard clearly in Metro Manila, and his station is only half the international standard of frequency separation from the next station, 400 kilohertz instead of 800 kilohertz, by God, he is running interference in an area where he is not supposed to be. The Progressive Broadcasting Corporation and the Quest Broadcasting Inc. are right in lodging their complaints. The Kapisanan Ng Mga Brodkaster Ng Pilipinas (KBP) is right in adding its voice to the protest. Finally the National Telecommunications Commission (NTC) is right when it ordered Tito Ojeda to change his location or change his antenna to avoid being a pest and a pirate.
August 21, 2001

9. Perils of Eugenia Duran Apostol

Tis is a story that has been told before in Metro magazine and others, but somehow it does not do justice to Eugenia Duran Apostol, the spunky woman publisher who defied Marcos and founded the Inquirer, the most widely read newspaper today -- and defended it against corporate raiders who want to take it away from her. I wrote the story complete from beginning to the present, with the permission of Apostol, but it never saw print even in her own paper.

There was a time during the early postwar years when we UP engineering students marched like horny Romeos walking backwards, with slide-rules sticking out of back pockets like cocks of the morning.

Of the UP students then, the most recognizable were little Peping Apostol and tall Victor Lim, because together they looked like Mutt and Jeff, and the two were the only ones singing the National Anthem out of beat and out of tune.

We at the Tau Alpha frat were laying bets that our brod Peping would one day marry a Big Fat Mamma, so imagine our surprise when he married the pretty petite aspiring journalist Eugenia Duran of Holy Ghost College.

This was the first of The Perils of Eugenia, marrying a Romeo who walked backwards and who sang out of tune and out of beat, so it seemed to us -- Vic Lim, Wallace Moran, Fedi Maramba, Dante Santos, JV Cruz and our wives -- who sang Christmas carols with them in the late 50's. She survived the slings and arrows of outrageous fortune only to face the whips and scorns of time -- one danger after the other, like the old movie serial, The Perils of Pauline.

The Perils of Pauline (1914) was one of the first and the greatest of movie serials that proliferated up to World War II, in which for 15 minutes every Thursday, for 12 episodes or chapters, the heroine undergoes plane wrecks, fire at sea, train wrecks, car crashes, being tied to the railroad track on the path of a speeding locomotive, and always get saved in the last minute.

Now that is the kind of life led by Eugenia "Eggie" Duran Apostol, founder and publisher of Mr&Ms and Philippine Daily Inquirer.

The second episode in the life of Eggie was soon after the death of Ninoy Aquino. On the very day of his funeral, Eggie printed the first of her weekly Mr&Ms Special Editions, which peaked at 500,000 copies per issue, chronicling the uphill battle against Marcos and the trial of the Ninoy-Galman murders.

Marcos had her on top of the list of those to be liquidated at the close of Martial Law, but she had a not-so-secret ally, then Defense Minister Juan Ponce Enrile.

The third episode was when during the Snap elections, she joined hands with Betty Go-Belmonte to set up The Philippine Daily Inquirer to help Cory win the election. At one time, during the Cory boycott the Inquirer (300,000 copies a day) outsold the crony paper Bulletin Today (200,000 copies daily).

This episode ended when Bible Betty fingered a passage in the Book saying that she will set up a new paper with three men (Max Sullivan, Art Borjal and Tony Roces), and so she left the Inquirer, Eggie and His Immensity Luis Beltran, without a press, and set up her own Philippine Star.

The fourth episode in The Perils of Eugenia was when she bidded for the two presses of the Daily Express, and won both with the highest bid, only to have the PCGG award one of the presses to the Lopez's Chronicle.

Eggie needed P10 million to pay for the press, and borrowed the same from First Pacific Capital. Despite the fact that Inquirer was only second to Bulletin, Eggie decided to sell out to the Soriano interests (of San Miguel Corporation) when she found out that the staffers did not want the cooperative and might opt for a labor union.

Editor Louie Beltran got involved in a fight with Joker Arroyo, and in an argument with Eggie and Letty Magsanoc over the use of the front page against Joker, made *tampo*, and quit.

Soriano got into a fight with the PCGG over San Miguel, And Eggie found out that the Sorianos planned to invite Beltran back as Inquirer editor, so she backed out of the deal, and the Sorianos being involved in a public controversy, graciously consented.

The fifth episode came when the Inquirer staff decided that they would rather be employees entitled to collective bargaining, than owners of Inquirer entitled to cash dividends.

So Eggie told the Treasurer Danny Venida to buy back for the account of the company the shares of those who wanted to sell. In the meantime, Venida quietly bought for the account of his friends at the Opus Dei, and told Eggie, "Surprise, surprise, the Opus Dei now controls 53 percent of outstanding shares."

At this point, First Pacific which extended a loan at 12 percent per annum convertible to common shares, threatened to convert and drive the Opus Dei shares to a locked-in minority position.

The Opus Dei sold out to Eggie who then invited Mariano Quimson (lately of the Bulletin) and his associates to invest on the basis of equal shares with her. Later Quimson also bought out the First Pacific Loan.

The sixth episode consists of a court battle with Nora Bitong, surrogate of Juan Ponce Enrile who claims a 20 percent share of Mr&Ms and wants a share of Inquirer for Mr&Ms.

The seventh episode is the court battle with Mariano Quimson who claims that 1,760 of Eggie's shares in Inquirer was paid with company funds (even when Eggie was advancing most of the working capital) and therefore must revert to treasury stock. Is Eggie going to lose control of Inquirer?
Watch for the sensational concluding episode of this thrilling chapter-play.

Eggie keeps control of the Inquirer

As of today, Eggie Duran Apostol won the first round of her case before the SEC when the hearing officers granted her petition for three injunctions against Mariano Quimson: to restore her shares, put her back as chairman, and back in control of the Inquirer.

After having been relieved of her position as chairman by an unexpected move by her partner Quimson disenfranchising 1,760 of her 44,000 shares, Eggie finally retrieved control of her paper with the three SEC injunctions.

She has 49 percent of the outstanding shares, and Mar has another 49 percent. The two percent minority which declared support for Eggie is now the swing vote that will decide the composition of the board and the management of the Inquirer.

Of course, Quimson is expected to appeal the decision to the SEC en banc but he has no longer the advantage of the status quo.

I owe Eggie Apostol my career in journalism. She taught me the rudiments of advocacy journalism, protecting me from religious freaks, frustrated biddies, greedy oligarchs, Cory Cronies, colonial assholes, neanderthal Americans -- who wanted me fired.

She said the readers are our bosses, not the advertisers or the powers-that-be. If my column is read, if we have a large readership, the advertisers will follow, and the powers will respect us.

She was right. Despite the departure of columnists Max Sullivan, Borjal and Beltran, Inquirer increased its circulation to within a whisker behind Bulletin, and sold three times more copies than Bulletin does in the provinces. Inquirer now claims to be Number One.

Now you see what Nora Bitong, Juan Ponce Enrile and Mar Quimson are quarreling with Eggie for -- a newspaper of high circulation and great influence in the contemporary scene.

Whatever happened to the friendship between Eggie Apostol and Juan Ponce Enrile? The friendship started when Johnny E had two houses built by Eggie's husband, Peping Apostol, who is well-established in construction and civil works. Johnny and wife Cristina took a liking to Eggie and Peping, and invited them often to Cristina's fabulous parties and to play mahjong.

Eggie was then the editor of the women's section of the Manila Chronicle, went on to edit Woman's Home Companion, and quit.

It was then that she set up the Mr&Ms magazine, with the 20 percent participation of friend Cristina Ponce Enrile.

When Eggie decided to launch her weekly Mr&Ms Special Edition after Ninoy was assassinated, the participation of Ponce Enrile in the paper was deliberately kept secret, since Enrile was still Marcos' defense secretary.

When Eggie set up the Inquirer as a cooperative among staff members, Enrile who as a government official did not want to be involved, encouraged it, so Eggie believed. Enrile was advised of the plan for the cooperative to buy the name Philippine Inquirer from Mr&Ms.

The trouble started when the Inquirer began to be critical of Defense Secretary Ponce Enrile in his tiff with President Cory Aquino. Taking offense, Enrile dropped the Apostols from his guest list and circle of friends, and eventually took Eggie to court.

Nora Bitong, surrogate of Juan Ponce Enrile, claims that the Inquirer was launched with a million peso loan from Mr&Ms of which she is 20 percent owner. Therefore she should have the same opportunity as Eggie (who owns 49 percent) to own 10 percent of the Inquirer, in proportion to her Mr&Ms holdings.

Eggie claims it was a loan personally guaranteed by her and long paid back with interest, and Bitong and Enrile never shared the risk she took. The loan was extended to the Inquirer to help it over the payrolls (Bible Betty provided the press), until it could be made into a cooperative for newspapermen, which did not come to pass because they preferred to organize as labor union, and later when Venida quietly acquired the majority for his Opus friends.

And that, my friends, is the sixth episode in the continuing story of The Perils of Eugenia.

Now for the seventh episode. Mar Quimson claims that 1,760 out of the 44,000 shares of Eggie, was paid for by the Company, should therefore revert to Treasury Stock (owned by Inquirer, not Eggie). This puts Eggie definitely in the minority.

Eggie denied the charge, and claims that it was paid in cash, or that it was paid out of the big loans she extended to the Inquirer. Nevertheless, to end the controversy, she paid P176,000 in check to the corporation that was never cashed.

She claims further that this is a moot question anyway because Mar and she have an agreement always to have the same number of shares even if he converts the First Pacific loan to equity. Eggie must be issued new shares to equalize the difference. What agreement? asks Mar Quimson. Atty. Dodo Ayuyao, corporation counsel, offers proof of such agreement.

Eggie would lose control of the Inquirer if 1,760 of her 44,000 shares were not allowed to vote. Furthermore, two extra directors appointed to represent the creditors (then the First Pacific, and now the Quimson group which bought the notes) would vote with Quimson's group so that Eggie would be outvoted in the board, if these two creditor-appointed directors were allowed to take sides in this fight for control between Quimson and Eggie.

According to Eggie's lawyers, these two directors should only be ex-officio directors and should be allowed to vote when the issue directly affects the capacity of the company to repay the loan. Also, that the board erred in disenfranchising her 1,760 shares which she bought in good faith, and which the Quimson group is challenging in bad faith, considering she herself invited Quimson to be her co-equal partner.

The board, dominated by Quimson and the creditor-appointed directors, declared all positions vacant, including the chairmanship of Eggie. Mar Quimson left for abroad on an vacation till January, and left the management to an Executive Committee of three.

And Eggie who founded the Inquirer suddenly found herself out in the cold, not allowed even to enter the newsroom, being asked to vacate her office space, and disauthorized even from suggesting where the next site of Inquirer should be (the present one was condemned and deemed unsafe after the last earthquake).

What Eggie's lawyers asked the SEC to do is to force the board to validate Eggie's payment for and recognize the voting rights of Eggie's 1,760 shares; to limit the voting powers of the creditor-appointed directors only to matters directly affecting their loan, and therefore to render them useless in a proxy fight; to order the reinstatement of Eggie as the Chairman of the Board, to revert the management back to the status quo; and to order an immediate stockholders'meeting.

Since Eggie and the Quimson group hold 49 percent each of the outstanding shares, the swing vote and deciding factor will be lodged in the minority of approximately two percent held by the staffers of the Inquirer. A majority of this group intervened in the suit on the ground that the Quimson take-over deprived the minority of its value as the deciding vote -- a situation that was planned from the inception of the paper.

It is expected that when the voting comes to a head, the minority will vote with Eggie.

Quimson appealed the decision to the SEC en banc which opted instead to get the parties together for an out-of-court settlement. As of now, though she is the chief executive officer, Eggie is still not in control of editorial policy or corporate affairs.

And an eighth episode is brewing now as the editor-in-chief who was appointed by Eggie herself and who was elected to the board with Eggie's votes, has aligned himself with Quimson against Eggie.

The legal questions are still to be resolved finally by the SEC and the courts. The cliff-hanger question is: will Eugenia Apostol weather the two latest assaults on her ownership of the paper she founded?

The Perils of Pauline, on which Eggie's life story seems to be based, always ends each episode with the heroine hanging by her fingernails in the face of disaster -- but in the end, Pauline always triumphs.

The question is, after having won the first round in the latest episode of the Perils of Eugenia Duran Apostol, will our heroine also triumph in the end?

September 19, 1993

Epilogue:

I was appointed Presidential Consultant on National Affairs by President Fidel Ramos in 1992, and resigned from the Philippine Inquirer. Eggie Apostol still had her problem at the Securities Exchange Commission under Perfecto Yasay. She realized that the battle for corporate control was detrimental to the paper she founded; Apostol severed all corporate and editorial ties with the Philippine Daily Inquirer on January 26, 1994, resigning from the board and retiring from the paper. The Inquirer was sold lock, stock and barrel to Marixi Prieto who promised to keep its editorial policies.

Apostol was awarded the Ramon Magsaysay Award for Journalism, Literature & Creative Communication Arts in 2006 in recognition of "her courageous example in placing the truth-telling press at the center of the struggle for democratic rights and better government in the Philippines".

In 2017, President Rodrigo Duterte, stung by the criticisms of the Inquirer ordered Marixi Prieto to vacate "MileLong" real estate along on Amorsolo street, after its government lease expired. To protect the Inquirer from politicians, Marixi sold the paper to Ramon Ang of San Miguel Corporation. *November 1, 2017*

10. Our AFP and gov't are run by comedians

That Rizal Alih is something, policeman and murderer, businessman and racketeer, political hack and tong-collector, and probably the most daring swashbuckler of our time and place.

When you come right down to it, Filipino Muslims are probably the best fighting men, pound for pound, man for man in the whole world, better than the Israelis. My uncle, who was involved in pre-war Moro campaigns, recounted stories of Muslim *juramentados* who bound their bodies tightly with a strip of cloth to keep their guts from spilling out. Then they ran amok, killing many Christians before they were themselves killed.

My uncle told of an American soldier who stood his ground with an Enfield rifle, pumping 30.06 caliber bullets into a Moro running towards him with a *kris* from yards away. The Moro never stopped or wavered, and as he came closer, the American fixed his bayonet, and charging, thrust it into the Moro's chest.

The Moro took hold of the Enfield rifle with his left hand, thrust it deeper into his own chest, and with his right hand swung his *kris* toward the American. My uncle with a shudder recalled, "For a moment, the American stood there headless, while his head hung from his neck by a strip of skin. Then both fell in the dust."

John Joseph Pershing fresh from the Indian wars against the Apaches and Sioux, and the Cuban campaign against the Spaniards, was sent here by President Theodore Roosevelt to pacify the Moros. The .45 caliber pistol with a wallop of a mule was invented to subdue the Moro, but to no avail. Pershing figured that "the only good Moro is a dead one," and proceeded to make Muslim Mindanao a howling wilderness, the pictorial proof of which is available in the Library of Congress.

So successful was Pershing that he was promoted from captain to brigadier general over 862 officers, entrusted with a punitive force (against international law) to pursue Pancho Villa into Mexico, and given the command of the American Expeditionary Army to Europe in World War I. In 1919, he was given the permanent rank of general, a grade previously held only by Washington, Grant, Sherman and Sheridan.

As far as our Armed Forces are concerned, let's face it, they are a big joke -- the only things they are good at are shooting at unarmed people who cannot shoot back: students, priests, nuns and concerned women, peasant families sleeping in the dead of night, workers and labor leaders walking the streets, nationalists like Ninoy Aquino shot at the back of the head -- not to mention carnapping, bankrobbing, and escorting smuggled goods. These jokers are only good for disseminating McCarthyist dung from the colon of CIA Chief Billygoat Lofgren: from a news-leak that communist cadres infiltrated the Congress, to the allegation that nuns and bishops are Communist dupes.

Against our real enemies they are useless. Pit the Army against one armed goon like Rizal Alih, or one charlatan like Gringo Honasan, or General Baula and Ka Roger -- and our soldiers stumble and fumble and fall over each other like the Keystone Cops chasing Charlie Chaplin. With all the modern weapons in the world, and a 10-to-one numerical superiority over the rebels, they are about as effective as Lilliputans against Gulliver.

During the attack on Alih, the army announced that the operation was called off on account of darkness. Holy Dung, they think it's a baseball game!

What do you do about police forces who can not enforce a firecracker ban, and whose only solution is to legalize firecrackers? What do you think of an army who cannot control unlicensed firearms, and whose only recourse is to license them? Just like the Bimbo who cannot catch most illegal aliens, and suggests that we legalize them all. Just like the Banshee who cannot stomach smuggling, therefore legalized smuggling by import liberalization. Like the Bruja who cannot prevent the Army from violating human rights, and therefore depicts them as being the victims rather than the violators.

By God, we have a bunch of comedians running our government!

Face it, following the example and advice of Mommie Dearest America is a mistake. Even in peacetime, U.S.A. is the most violent in the world. In 1980, handguns killed 77 persons in Japan; 8 in Great Britain; 24 in Switzerland; 8 in Canada; 23 in

Israel; 18 in Sweden; 4 in Australia; and 11,522 in the United States.

We should follow the example of Costa Rica which abolished their army in their 1949 constitution, and never had any trouble from communists and carpetbaggers ever since, unlike its neighbors Nicaragua and Honduras.

January 14, 1989

11. Cory, give us a Vision, don't let Ninoy die!

Dear Cory, on primetime TV, one station after another, we see nothing but low comedy or rock variety show. We live in a frivolous society.

The great philosopher historian Arnold Toynbee once said that no great civilization ever declines from external forces alone. It first rots from within. It rots from within if it has no vision to illumine its path, no direction, no plan of action. It rots when its reason for being becomes frivolous, irrelevant, unimportant to the lives of its citizens.

Every great administration has a slogan to crystallize its vision. US president McKinley had his Manifest Destiny; Roosevelt his New Deal; Kennedy, New Frontier; Johnson, Great Society. Magsaysay had his Common Man; Garcia his Filipino First; Macapagal, Unfinished Revolution; Marcos, A Nation Great Again and Bagong Lipunan.

What is ours, dear Cory?

Cory, Cory, Cory?

Once in a while, at a high point of history, a great symbol comes into being, it becomes a rallying point. We had one such symbol, like the blazing sign in the heavens by which Constantine was told: In hoc signo, vinces!

It is the martyrdom of Ninoy Aquino. By this sign we did conquer the unconquerable at Edsa. Where is Ninoy today?

Last August 21, on the 4th anniversary of Ninoy's martyrdom, only Cecile Guidote Alvarez remembered, as she planned out the week's activities. On the tarmac where Ninoy was killed, a program was set, and only 20 people attended, mostly the diplomatic corps. At the Sto. Domingo Church, where millions once attended the funeral mass, the memorial mass this year barely filled half the church. At the newly inaugurated Ninoy Aquino Park in Quezon City, the program attracted about 800 people in the amphitheater.

Is Ninoy the Symbol already dead, Cory?

"Why Ninoy?" asked Marcos once, and I answered to his face in front of his wife Imelda, "Ninoy alive was vulnerable because he was only human. Ninoy dead is invincible because he has become the focus of all the glorious things that might have been, a rallying point, a symbol of hope and national unity."

Don't let Ninoy die, Cory!

Our only salvation, Cory, lies in the strength of our institutions, the more important being the army, police, and our schools. The army and the police are important because people depend on them for protection. When the NPA, the MNLF and criminal elements violate the people's human rights, it is a serious crime and the army and police must punish them. When the army and the police violate the people's human rights, it is much much more than a serious crime, it is a BETRAYAL of the people's trust. No one else can punish them. The army and the police are being paid to protect us, to uphold the full majesty of the law.

But who will protect us from our protectors when they themselves violate our human rights??

There is NO protection. The police and the army, when they commit crimes against us, are the same ones who investigate the crimes and track down the guilty -- and that is why the murders of Ninoy, Lando Olalia and Lean Alejandro will never be solved. That is why, dear Cory, all the demands of the army and the police for "equal treatment" in the prosecution of human rights violations, of amnesty and forgiveness for Honasan, and "formal negotiations" between Honasan and the government -- sound hollow.

We are paying the military to give us security, not to decide our destiny. We paid for the education of Honasan and his ilk, we paid for their uniforms, guns and salaries. And we trusted them to protect us. When the military commits an abuse, it is not just a crime, it is a betrayal of trust, it is TREASON. That is why it is important, dear Cory, that the National Defense secretary be a civilian and a constitutionalist, to emphasize civilian supremacy and adherence to the constitution and the law. Ex-Justice Vicente Abad Santos, Solicitor General Frank Chavez, Joker Arroyo, Francis Garchitorena -- any would make a great defense secretary.

Even more important is the Department of Education. In every barangay in the Philippines, where policemen are feared, mistrusted or simply non-existent, there is a teacher who is ever present and respected. Schools are everywhere. There are state colleges in Baguio for the Cordilleras people, in Marawi where the Muslims are, and everywhere where NPA leaders have their early education and their first experience in mass action. Why then do our children prefer to be citizens of the USA or Saudi than of their own country, according to a UP survey? Because our mentors have no vision, no direction, no sense of history.

You complain, dear Cory, of the fact that your Cabinet members cannot work together. How could they if they have no shared vision, no grand design that only you can provide?

Alejandro Roces was the best education secretary we ever had because he has a sense of history and a vision of the future. But then he may not even want to join your cabinet.

Arnold Toynbee concluded that history is a series of challenges and responses, that a nation falls when its leaders fail to respond frontally to a series of challenges.

Dear Cory, you've undergone five attempted coups by disgruntled soldiers, with the covert participation of the CIA -- and each time you appease them by moving further to the right of the political spectrum. You have received five punches without retaliating; you are encouraging them to follow up with a 6th knockout blow.

Again and again, the Council of Trent compromised our interests in favor of foreign banks, IMF and multinationals -- and each time you give in... and move away from self-reliance and industrialization, back to the plantation type of colonial economy.

Dear Cory, give us a vision of the future, a Grand Design. Respond frontally to the challenge.

And dear Cory, don't let Ninoy die.

September 29, 1987

12. Cory 'made Indian' to Malcolm Forbes

What? Cory canceled a meeting with Malcolm S. Forbes, billionaire publisher of the business magazine Forbes (the world's number one), along with seven of his billionaire friends?

Nakakahiya, says a Councilor of Trent who was in the presidential party, "This was a meeting arranged at the initiative of Malacañang, not Forbes, three months ago. And Forbes was honored and enthusiastic, how could we do this to the most powerful man in the US business community?"

"I haven't heard one good excuse for this sudden change of plans," said one government official who looks like a cardinal with a lopsided smile.

"It is embarrassing," an irritated source at the Forbes Building on Fifth Ave. said, "Invitations had been sent out. People responded to the invitation by Mr. Forbes and it was canceled at the last minute."

Indeed, our US public relations firm, The Sawyer Miller Group, encouraged the meeting between Cory and Malcolm Forbes, knowing that Forbes'visit to Thailand generated excitement for that country as a tourist destination, and that his 70th birthday bash in Morocco in which he spent $2 million and flew his guests in his 727 Boeing jet reportedly generated interest in building first-class hotels.

Who is Malcolm Forbes?

Well, he is the dream boy of the Council of Trent, members of the presidential party who had long wanted to shake hands and hobnob with the real Rich and Famous, even if it means using our President Cory to provide the occasion. Said their PR: "It is important that the president is seen courting US businessmen like Forbes." Indeed.

Who is Malcolm Forbes?

He is the current flame of ex-superstar, the once beautiful Elizabeth Taylor. He is one of the hundreds welcomed into her bed, although it boggles the imagination to picture a 70-year old blown-out fuse perform with an old fat lady.

Malcolm Forbes wanted the Cory meeting on his yacht. Malacañang said no. Finally it was agreed that the meeting should take place in the New York office of Forbes, although this violates protocol. Forbes and friends should call on our head of state, not vice versa.

Twenty-three invitations were sent out by Forbes, but only seven accepted -- an indication of the low regard for our social-climbing Council of Trent by the really Rich and Famous of America.

Contrast this with Cory's visit (arranged by PNB and Lilia Calderon Clemente) to the New York Stock Exchange which sent out 57 invitations to the heads of the biggest US corporations, out of which 47 attended that wonderful affair where our credit-standing as a nation was proven to the world.

The Forbes meeting was canceled a week before from Manila, not "at the last minute" as complained by a disappointed Trentist.

The Forbes meeting was the brainchild of three noodle brains: Trade Sec. Jose Concepcion, lusting as usual for Forbes' Proscuito ham; Tourist Sec. Peter Garrucho as tourist wanting to meet with Elizabeth Taylor; and Sec. Ping the Jesus, head of the advance party.

These Three Stooges must have fallen on their knees to beg the great Malcolm Forbes for an audience with President Cory, promising to get Don Jaime Zobel de Ayala to rename Forbes Park after him.

The original Forbes Park was named by the Ayalas after Cameron Forbes, a brainless Bostonian who became our Governor General, known to Quezon and Osmeña for lack of intelligence and excess of arrogance.

Who were the seven guests of Malcolm Forbes that the Councilors of Trent wanted so much to meet?

Among them, ha ha ha ha:

The doddering old Laurence Rockefeller, 79, one of the two surviving children of John D. Rockefeller Jr. (the other is David, 74) -- both worth a total of $1.6 billion. John D. Jr. is the son of robber baron John D. Sr., the world's first billionaire who built Standard Oil out of the bones of so many small oil companies.

In self defense, Congress passed the Sherman Anti-Trust Law by which the Rockefeller monopoly was broken up into 32 corporations, six of which are still among the biggest in the world.

The clan wealth is dispersed to 22 great grandchildren headed by David Jr. who just sold the Rockefeller Plaza to the Japanese. They are selling, not buying, so why will they invest in the Philippines?

Leonard and Ronald Lauder, the two sons of billionaire Este Lauder ($2 billion), manufacturer of cosmetics. Ronald spent an unprecedented $12 million in an election he lost to New York Mayor Koch. How will they invest here, as a licensee of *Katialis*?

Leonard Norman Stern ($1.5 billion), manufacturer of bird seeds and pet supplies, hardly the type we need in our country, unless it is the only way we can feed our starving population.

Ha ha ha ha ha, some guest list!
November 14, 1989

ooooo

FOREIGN POLICY IN CRISIS:

Part One: Do we have Exocet missiles?

Contrary to what Secretary Fidel Ramos says, the Philippines may actually have some deadly computer-guided French-made Exocet missiles. In the 1987 yearbook of the Stockholm International Peace Research Institute (SIPRI), page 260, the Philippines is shown to have purchased French-made "MM-38 Exocet Sh Sh Ms" and Swedish-made "Bofors 57 mm. gun" from the Republic of South Korea.

There the Malaysians were, boldly humiliating the Philippines, first by holding hostage 49 Filipinos, maltreating them till one died of heart attack, then by reportedly intruding into our territory in the Sulu Sea triangle at least six times from January to August this year -- now our Secretary of Defense Fidel Ramos says our navy is too weak to resist a Malaysian invasion in the disputed territories.

The Malaysian navy is reputed to have some French-made Exocet missles, the same that sunk a British battleship during the Falkland war; and Ramos says we do not have any.

The military forces of the Malaysian Federation, according to our intelligence agencies, are about as effective as our ROTC units in our colleges, our navy almost equal to theirs and strong enough to repel sea-borne invaders. So why do our Armed Forces pretend that they cannot perform their duty to protect our territory?

Are they actually goading the Malaysians into an invasion in which the Malaysian forces will eventually get a bloody nose?

Are they baiting the Congress of the Philippines to give them a hefty budgetary increase?

Are they being influenced by the American CIA or the British MI6 to put a wet blanket on any bold initiatives of the Dept. of Foreign Affairs?

Are they being asked by the CIA to provoke the Malaysians into attacking to provide an excuse for the American Marines to land and intervene in in our internal affairs like in Vietnam?

Or are they just cowards, yellow-bellies, poltroons -- good only for massacring unarmed laborers, students, peasants and priests??

The fact is that our Foreign Policy is in crisis:

o Malaysia is pressuring the Philippines to drop the Sabah Claim, with an implied threat to sever relations and doom the ASEAN to extinction.

o Malaysia is at the same time provoking the Philippines with border incidents in the Kalayaan Island group west of Palawan, and in the Sulu Sea Triangle of the Turtle Islands near Sandakan, Sabah.

o Malaysia, having helped create the MNLF, is providing arms, sanctuary and rest-and-rehabilitation areas for the MNLF insurgents in the Sabah area.

o The possibility of war by miscalculation is frightening.

o The United States is poised to neglect its obligations to come to our aid under our Mutual Defense Treaty if we are invaded by Malaysia.

o Talks have been scheduled between Malaysia and the Philippines, and we are not ready, the prospects of a comic opera foul-up approaching by the minute.

To reach as wide an audience as possible and to involve our people in our Foreign Affairs -- this series of articles on our Foreign Policy in Crisis will be written not like a solemn treatise, but as an informal narrative gleaned from frank conversations with Filipino diplomats, as we heard it, with wit, humor, self-deprecation, exaggeration, and wild surmise -- and always with a Filipino attitude of *bahala na* and great expectations. But it is true and very serious.

As originally conceived, the following articles will follow this first one: (2) Cloma, Arreglado, and their nation composed of only two citizens, now the focus of international dispute; (3) The Bombing of Turumba Laxamana, or why the Malaysians are raring to get even; (4) Comic Opera in our Sabah negotiations, past and present, or the Deaf, the Drunk and the Confused; (5) Alex Melchor as Henry Kissinger, and a special souvenir for President Bongo of Gabon; (6) Tripoli Agreement, in the name of God the Most Compassionate and Merciful; (7) The Jeddah Accords, a whole new ballgame with Nur Misuari; (8) Letty versus her Papa on Sabah, or Our Claim in retrospect; (9) A serious Summing Up.

The series may be reworked and re-scheduled according the pressure of current events.

Part Two: Cloma, Arreglado: the only citizens of Freedomland
West of Palawan, in the South China Sea, are a group of islands that was first thought to be part of the Spratlys, now a subject of overlapping claims by China, Vietnam, Taipei, Malaysia and the Philippines. Our claim to it originated with a hail-fellow-well-met curly-mopped self-styled Admiral of the Seven Seas, named Tomas Cloma.

Tomas Cloma was the founder, owner, and President of the Philippine Nautical School which operated a training ship built from a war surplus Liberty Ship. In 1956 while on a training voyage as an "Admiral" on board his ship in the South China Sea, he encountered a storm that drove his ship off course to a big uninhabited island where he sought refuge.

Consulting his navigational maps, he found that the island belonged to a group of islets occupied by the Japanese during World War II, as a base from which to attack commercial shipping in the South China Sea.

Despite his primitive knowledge of International Law, Cloma's Boholano heritage moved him to do a Sikatuna, proclaiming himself King of these islands he now baptized Freedomland.

Upon his return to Manila, Admiral Cloma called on fellow Boholano, Vice President and Foreign Affairs Secretary Carlos P. Garcia, asking him to send formal notices to the whole world and the United Nations on behalf of Freedomland. President Magsaysay and the rest of the nation thought it was all a joke.

Vice President Garcia, soon to be president upon the death of Magsaysay, did not want any fellow Boholano to be a king, a position higher than his own, so he sent Cloma with a ha-ha-ha to the legal adviser of the Department of Foreign Affairs, Counselor Juan Arreglado.

Since Juan Arreglado had megalomaniac tendencies of his own, he asked Tomas Cloma to appoint him Prime Minister and Foreign Minister (like his fellow Bantangueño Doy Laurel once was just after EDSA) of Freedomland. In this capacity, he drafted all the international documents to perfect the claim of Cloma on Freedomland and legitimize their status as King and Prime Minister respectively of a nation made up of exactly two citizens and a thousand turtles.

For a long time, King Tomas I and his Prime Minister Arreglado were the laughing stock of the diplomatic corps. But that was before traces of oil were found off the shore of Palawan in the same geological formation as was Freedomland. All of a sudden the possibility of oil finds, as proven in the 1976 Matinloc and Cadlao oil discoveries, made Freedomland a potential source of precious oil.

In 1972, when Martial Law was declared, Defense Secretary Juan Ponce Enrile sent his soldiers to arrest and detain Tomas Cloma in Camp Aguinaldo, and at the same time called Juan Arreglado to appear for questioning at Camp Crame.

Secretary Enrile accused King Tomas Cloma and Prime Minister Juan Arreglado of usurpation of public office and illegal use of titles.

Secretary Enrile was not joking, he was dead serious. Hailed before a military tribunal, Tomas Cloma was forbidden ever to use the title Admiral and King, and Juan Arreglado who previously was Ambassador to Korea and Egypt, was forbidden to use the title of Prime Minister and Foreign Minister.

And just to make sure that the message was loud and clear to all, Presidential Decree 1596, proclaimed by President Ferdinand Marcos on June 11, 1978, legally annexed Freedomland to the Philippines, and renamed it the Kalayaan group.

It was over this Kalayaan group, that the Philippines almost went to war with Malaysia in 1980, in an incident called the Bombing of Turumbu Laxamana, starring a gung-ho Navy Commander Gil Fernandez (not related to Jobo), and a young Navy Captain Carlito Cunanan, whose act of war humiliated the Malaysians and made them vow revenge someday.

It is suspected that the ascension of now Admiral Carlito Cunanan to the post of FOIC, Flag Officer in Command of the Philippine Navy, has triggered memories of long ago and led to the detention of three Filipino vessels with its 49-member crew in the Turumbu Laxamana island where Malaysia was humiliated eight years ago.

Tomorrow we shall tell the story of the Bombing of Turumbu Laxamana.

Part Three: The Bombing of Turumbu Laxamana

West of Palawan in the South China Sea, there is this tiny islet identified in International Maps as Commodore Reef. In Philippine maps it is called Rizal Reef. In Malaysian maps it is called "Turumbu Laxamana" translated in Bahasa Malayu as "Powerful Admiral." This islet almost figured in a war between Malaysia and the Philippines.

On June 11, 1978, President Ferdinand Marcos issued Presidential Decree 1597, defining Tomas Cloma's Freedomland as Philippine territory -- now renamed The Kalayaan Group, of which Rizal's Reef was part, the other major islands being Pag-asa, Patag, Panata, Likas, Ligao, Luna Reef, etcetera.

Because there is a possibility that oil resources may exist in these islands, Marcos issued on the same day, another Presidential Decree number 1599, declaring and defining an Exclusive Economic Zone (EEZ) as per the Law of the Sea, extending 200 miles off Palawan, to ensure that any offshore oil producing areas in the Kalayaan Group, are within the exclusive sovereignty of the Philippines.

And to further strengthen Philippine proprietary rights, on the same day Marcos promulgated Presidential Proclamation # 370, to define the continental shelf of the Philippines to extend as far southwest to the island the Malaysians call Turumbu Laxamana.

Subsequently, the Malaysians issued new maps showing the Rizal Reef known to them as Turumbu Laxamana, to be Malaysian Territory.

It is a barren reef that suddenly became important because oil deposits seem to exist in the continental shelf of which Rizal Reef and Palawan were part. The Malaysian Marines once landed there but left because of the rough seas which made the place uninhabitable most of the year, especially during the monsoon season. "Only crazy Filipinos can live there," said a Malaysian diplomat.

When Philippine National Oil Co. (PNOC) under Energy Minister Ronnie Velasco decided to explore for oil in the Kalayaan, and in view of the fact that the territories were subjected to overlapping claims by China, Vietnam, Taipei and Malaysia, President Marcos decided to create the Western Command of the Armed Forces with responsibility to police the area.

He chose as the head of the Western Command, our toughest Navy Commander, Commodore Gil Fernandez. He was actually hitting two birds with one stone. Commodore Fernandez, no kin to CB Governor Jobo Fernandez, was a "gung-ho type with big balls" who as Commander of the Southern Command went on a search-and-destroy mission that practically sent all Muslims within range to the embrace of Allah and the *houris*, the beautiful maidens who minister to the physical needs of those managing to reach the Muslim heaven. The Muslims did not appreciate this act of accommodation by Commodore Fernandez, and demanded that he be relieved. Marcos welcomed the opportunity to sic this Rambo on the Muslim Malaysians.

In 1980, while reconnoitering with his flagship over his new theater of command, Commodore Gil Fernandez spotted on Rizal Reef (Turumbu Laxamana) what looked like the Rizal Monument in the Luneta. Investigating he found it to be a concrete pylon marker with Malaysian markings that proclaimed the island of Turumbu Laxamana as part of the territory of Malaysia.   It was indeed as large as the Rizal Monument, with a large Malaysian flag waving above it.

Incensed, Commodore Fernandez went to Malacañang and asked the permission of Marcos to destroy the marker. Marcos as usual did not say yes or no, but gave him a look and a wink that Fernandez interpreted to mean "go ahead, Geronimo and gung-ho!"

Intent on liberating Philippine territory from Malaysian desecration, Commodore Fernandez set out with his young second-in-command Navy Captain Carlito Cunanan, a graduate of the US Naval Academy at Annapolis, the alma mater of Opus Dei Ambassador to Moscow, Alex Melchor.

On second thought, not being sure he interpreted Marcos' wink rightly, Commodore Francisco retreated with his flagship three nautical miles away from the shore of Turumbu Laxamana, and sent Navy Captain Carlito Cunanan to shore with a chest full of explosives.

Cunanan mined the Malaysian monument and blew it to smithereens in what Commodore Fernandez described as a "mini-Hiroshima" explosion. And to prove it, Cunanan and Fernandez had the whole shebang immortalized on videotape, showing it to all and sundry, to anyone who can organize a beer-and-chicharon party.

The videotape was called the Bombing of Turumbo Laxamana, and was inevitably circulated among the diplomatic corps, as a sort of tribute to Fernandez and Cunanan, as the nation's Rambo and Dirty Harry respectively.

In addition, a Filipino marine detachment was dispatched to Kalayaan in civilian clothes as fishermen, to satisfy an international law requirement of peaceful occupation of territory, to perfect a claim of national sovereignty over "*terra nullius*," an unoccupied land.

This embarrassed, irritated, and finally enraged the Malaysian naval attaches who swore that when the time comes, the Malaysian Navy will exact its full vengeance.

What drove the Malaysians to madness was when Prime Minister Cesar Virata, in the only military function Marcos allowed him to do, went to the Kalayaan Group and had himself photographed in full combat gear on top of a Bofor naval cannon pointed at the direction of Kuala Lumpur. After the picture was published, China, Vietnam and Malaysian filed a verbal protest in the Foreign Affairs Dept.

And revenge finally came, when to embarrass the newly installed Rear Admiral Carlito Cunanan, Flag Officer in Command of the Philippine Navy (FOIC) and Philippine Commander of the American Subic Naval Base, the Malaysian Navy attacked and captured three unarmed Filipino fishing vessels under air cover of helicopter gunships and arrested their 49 crew members, in Turumbo Laxamana, the very place where they suffered humiliation eight long years ago. According to official sources, the commander of the Malaysian Patrol thought that the three ships were part of an invasion fleet poised to occupy Malaysian territory. Revenge was sweet indeed.

In the meantime, gung-ho Commodore Gil Fernandez, now Vice President for Academic Affairs in the National Defense College, after presiding over the graduation of "General" TingTing Cojuangco, now dons his old Admiral's cap in anticipation of being promoted Admiral with three stars, so that he may outrank Rear Admiral Cunanan who is in the doghouse for allowing Gringo Honasan to escape. He expects to be sent back to Turumbu Laxamana, to blast the Malaysians out of the China Sea.

Part Four: Comic Opera negotiations on Sabah

So how is the Department of Foreign Affairs responding to the present crisis? Who will negotiate for us in the coming talks with Malaysia?

Ambassador Rodolfo Severino, who is the most experienced, having been till recently head of the Office of Asian and Pacific Affairs, is completely demoralized due to the tortuous gauntlet he is going through in the Commission on Appointments. Because his staff idolizes him, they too are demoralized.

His replacement, Ambassador Rora Navarro Tolentino, the daughter of Surigao's political kingpin Constantino "Oguing" Navarro is no doubt a brilliant law graduate of UP, but she has absolutely no experience in diplomatic negotiations, much less in the management of a major bilateral territorial conflict. She does not even know if Malaysia signed the Law of the Sea Convention or not.

On the other hand, retired Justice of Appeals Jorge Coquia (a bucayo from Pangasinan, considered Sen. Letty Shahani's protege) is no doubt a good scholar, having been co-author of a book on International Law together with CID Commissioner Miriam Defensor Santiago (a recent Magsaysay Awardee). Unfortunately Assistant Secretary for legal affairs Coquia is hard of hearing, and being a frugal Ilocano, does not care to buy the best and most expensive hearing aid.

During inter-office meetings, this Ilocano from the Catholic University in Washington DC, has been observed to remove his hearing aid, tapping it on the table to revive its failing power. So it has been a source of serious concern that Asst. Sec. Coquia is now designated head of our delegation in the coming talks with the Malaysians.

Imagine sending Jorge Coquia, with his thick Ilocano accent and failing faculty for hearing, to seriously negotiate with young, articulate, crafty and devious Malaysian diplomats trained in Oxford and Cambridge, only in their 40s and utterly contemptuous of even Harvard graduates (considered by the British as Colonials), and especially of UP and Ateneo graduates (considered by British-trained Malaysians as Colonials of Colonials, one step away from being complete barbarians).

One can imagine a complete re-enactment of the disastrous Bangkok Talks on Sabah in 1967, when we fielded another old man hard of hearing, the late Ambassador Eduardo Quintero (remember him? he exposed Marcos' corruption of the 1971 ConCon). It was comic opera all the way.

On the negotiating table, after having heard the opening statement of Malaysia's Deputy Minister Tan Sri Mohammed Ghazali bin Shaffie, brilliant and dripping with sarcasm, with a British accent reminiscent of Sir Laurence Olivier -- our Ambassador Quintero, who could not hear half of what Ghazali said, and could not understand the other half, simply developed cold feet, nervous diarrhea, complicated with an outsized inferiority complex. After the first session he cabled Manila asking for permission to go home, on the pretext that he left some documents in his safe.

His colleagues at the department knew he was scared of tangling with the brilliant Ghazali, because instead of taking the plane for the three-hour ride to Manila, Quintero chose to wait for an ocean freighter that took four days to reach Manila, and feigning illness, simply refused to go back to Bangkok.

In the meantime, Quintero's deputy with the improbable and ridiculous French name of Gauttier Bisnar, continued the talks. Gauttier came from Capiz and could hardly speak English without a thick Ilonggo accent that Malaysian Minister Ghazali and his colleagues with their Oxford training, simply could not understand.

After ten days of unproductive talks, in which Minister Ghazali became increasingly irritated, frustrated and openly contemptuous, our Secretary of Justice Claudio "Dingdong" Teehankee in Manila, then Marcos' Crisis Manager on the Sabah Claim, cabled an SOS to the only Filipino he knew with a British accent, Ateneo's pride, Leon Maria Guerrero, Ambassador to the Court of St. James in Great Britain.

The late Ambassador Leonie Guerrero, *summa cum laude*, and author of the award-winning book on Rizal, "The First Filipino," was a perfect choice, but for the fact that he was overly fond of alcoholic spirits. In the 16-hour flight from London to Bangkok, he emptied the bar of the British Airways 707, and its wine-and-liquor store as well. Bleary-eyed, soused and suffering from the inevitable jet lag, Leonie staggered into the negotiating table in Bangkok, finally face to face with the brilliant Ghazali who looked at his sorry condition, and without batting an eyelash, declared:

"The Malaysian delegation hereby rejects irrevocably the Philippine claim to Sabah."

Leonie Guerrero, drunk or sober, never lost an argument since his college days in Ateneo. Still dazed from his jet lag and marathon bout with Bacchus, the God of Wine and hard liquor, Leonie unsteadily rose to his full height, and retorted in perfect Arrneow accent:

"And the Philippine delegation hereby rejects irrevocably the Malaysians' irrevocable rejection of the Philippine claim to Sabah!"

One can almost see History repeat itself in the near future with a sober but hard-of-hearing Asst. Sec. Jorge Coquia heading our delegation to the next negotiation, stuck with an old bargain-basement hearing aid -- and issuing an SOS to the top boss Secretary Raul Manglapus, Ateneo's pride, with his impeccable Arrneow accent, in an encore of our Comic Opera style of negotiating.

Part Five: Alex Melchor as Kissinger, Bongo's souvenir

In March 1972, the world was shaken by the unilateral act of the United States in getting the US dollar off the gold standard, a *balasubas* act that overnight reduced the US external debt down to four percent of its value. The OPEC subsequently raised the price of oil several times, cut off the oil supply of their enemies, and the Great World Recession was on.

From 1972 to 1974, the MNLF supported by Malaysia and Libya, had better weapons than our AFP, and was running rings around our soldiers. Then on October 17, 1973, came the shocker.

The OPEC countries who collectively have a monopoly of oil production, imposed an embargo on the Philippines, not only because the Philippines was a slavish client of the USA who was in turn a client of Israel, but especially because the Philippines was being accused of conducting a policy of genocide against the Muslims. Out of the 13 OPEC countries, 11 are members of the Organization of Islamic Conference (OIC), big brother to Muslims all over the world.

The embargo was lifted only when we sent our Ambassador Liningding Pangandaman to present his credentials to King Feisal of Saudi Arabia. The good Ambassador was able to convince the King that the oil embargo on the Philippines worked more hardships on the Muslims than on the Christians.

Saudi Arabia which was most influential in the OPEC, had the embargo lifted on condition that the Philippines hold talks with the MNLF for a peaceful solution to the Mindanao conflict. The embargo was lifted Dec. 23, 1973.

In June 1974, the OIC ministers met in Kuala Lumpur, adopted Resolution # 18, calling upon the Philippines to talk to the MNLF, and sent OIC Sec. Gen. Dr. Mohammed Tohamy of Egypt to deliver the resolution to Marcos. In January 1975, Marcos sent a delegation to the OIC headquarters in Jeddah where the talks were held.

Our delegation was composed of Executive Secretary Alex Melchor, Admiral Romulo Espaldon, Col. Jose Almonte (now head of EIIB economic intelligence for the Dept. of Finance), Ambassadors Pagandaman and Pacifico Castro, and the academes Dean Ruben Santos Cuyugan and Prof. Cesar Majul of UP. The MNLF panel was composed of Nur Misuari, Hashim Salamat, Judge Abdul Hamid Lucman, Abdul Rasad Asani, and Abdul Baki Abubakar.

For two weeks, the MNLF demanded independence for the Bangsamoro Islamic Republic, but was rejected outright. The Philippine panel went to Libya to seek the help of Moamar Gaddafi, the chief bank-roller of the MNLF, then went on to Egypt to seek the help of President Anwar Sadat and Prime Minister Hegazy.

A special plane PAF C-130 (the same type in which Prime Minister Zia Ul-Haq of Pakistan recently died) was assigned to the Philippine delegation for its shuttle diplomacy. Secretary Alex Melchor head of the delegation began to imagine he was Henry Kissinger who was then on a shuttle diplomacy of his own. It was hilarious to watch Melchor with his ridiculous US midwestern twang, attempt to fake the accent of a German Jew.

But the Melchor Mission was inconclusive because his approach and methodology was purely academic, devised by the UP academes. So Alex Melchor in the thick Yiddish accent of Kissinger, asked Ambassador Pex Castro who is known among the Muslims as Castro the inFidel, to devise a new strategy which proved so simple and effective, even Marcos adopted it.

Looking at the composition of the OIC, the inFidel made the following observations:

o In the OIC, there are three groups: nine from Asia, 14 from the Arab bloc, and 23 from Africa.

o They are also divided by language groups: Arabic, English-speaking and Francophone (French-speaking).

o Misuari's MNLF was strong among the Asians who were English-speaking and understood their propaganda.

o The MNLF was also strong among the Arabs, because Filipino Muslim leaders such as Hashim Salamat and Abdul Baki Abubakar were graduates of the famous centuries-old (since the ninth century, and older than Sorbonne, the oldest in Western Europe) Al-Azar University in Cairo, which is the cultural center of the Arab world.

o But Misuari had absolutely no influence among the French-speaking Islamic Africans, who have a deep-rooted resentment against the Arabs, who were once the slave-traders who sold the blacks into slavery.

The French-speaking Francophone, Ambassador Pex Castro the inFidel suggested that the Philippines concentrate its attention in cultivating the friendship of the Black African Muslims.

The inFidel was right. In Dakar, Senegal, there is an island where in the 17th to the 19th centuries, Portuguese, French, Dutch and English slave ships would dock, to purchase black African slaves from Arab slave traders, who raided African villages in the coasts and far into the interior to capture men, women and children like horses and cattle for use in the New World. Black Africa has this trauma etched in its racial memory.

The inFidel was right. This policy proved effective when Marcos invited President Omar Bongo of Gabon, Africa, a member of OPEC and the OIC, to come to Manila for a State Visit in August 1976. President Bongo was completely won over by the Filipinos, specially one particular Filipina. Marcos endowed him with the highest decoration, the Order of Sikatuna, rank of Rajah. He was also given an honorary degree by the Far Eastern University, owned by the brother-in-law of President Cory Aquino.

President Omar Bongo made a speech proclaiming to the whole world that African Islamic States will reject the MNLF demand for secession.

And lugging all the prized souvenirs from the Philippines back to his capital city of Libreville, Gabon, President Bongo sent special envoys to all the capitals of the African member countries of OIC, to deliver letters from Bongo to his brother presidents, asking support for the territorial integrity of the Philippines. And that was what they did and are still doing, thanks to Bongo and the souvenir he brought along, escorted by Ambassador Monico Vicente.

Not only that, when the time came to send back the souvenir, courtesy of Mrs. Bongo, our dollar reserves became richer by $40,000.

Tomorrow we describe how we were trapped into the Tripoli Agreement

Part Six: Tripoli Agreement, in the name of God

On Friday last week, September 16, a meeting was held in Malacañang by the Mindanao Regional Consultative Council (RCC) to discuss a bill to be presented to Congress on Sept. 30, creating as per the Constitutional mandate, and according to the Tripoli Agreement, an autonomous region in Mindanao for the Muslims, to meet the constitution deadline on December 31, 1988.

This is the result of a train of events that started in July 1976, in Istanbul, Turkey, during the Foreign Ministers' Meeting of the Organization of Islamic Conference (OIC). Unfortunately our representative General Rafael "Rocky" Ileto, non-resident Philippine Ambassador to Turkey, was not in rapport with the local Turkish officials, so he was not able to move around enough to prevent the OIC from passing a resolution favorable to the MNLF.

In August 1976, the OIC Secretary General Dr. Amadou Karim Gaye of Senegal, accompanied by the Foreign Affairs Minister of Libya, Dr. Abdul Salam Ali Treki, came to Manila to deliver the OIC resolution, and to appeal to Marcos to resume negotiations with the MNLF. At the time, a big earthquake and huge tsunami (tidal wave) engulfed Mindanao, causing great damage and loss of life, a disaster that somehow created world-wide sympathy for our plight.

President Marcos agreed to send a delegation to meet the MNLF, upon the insistence of Foreign Minister Treki in Libya, North Africa. The Philippines did not at the time have any diplomatic relations with Libya, due of course to the influence of the USA which looked upon Libyan leader Gaddafi as a terrorist and devil incarnate. Marcos decided to remedy the situation by sending his wife Imelda on a goodwill mission to Gaddafi on November 1976.

Imelda always claimed she was the first to hold talks with Gaddafi, but it is not true, Alex "Henry Kissinger" Melchor was there before her. Neither did Imelda meet with any MNLF leader, she just charmed Gaddafi who developed a teen-age crush on her and tolerated her womanhood and extravagance, both restricted in his Fundamentalist Muslim state. In their talks, they agreed that a subministerial Philippine panel be sent to Tripoli to negotiate with the MNLF.

On December 7, 1976, Marcos sent a delegation composed of Defense Deputy Minister for Civilian Relations, the late Carmelo "Mike" Barbero as head of panel, Rear Admiral Romulo Espaldon, Col. Eduardo Ermita (now Defense undersecretary), Ambassadors Liningding Pangandaman and Pex Castro, Commissioner Simeon Datumanong, Southern Development Authority Administrator Karim Sidri. The latter, Karim Sidri, was a fake Muslim who is the son of Archive Director Domingo Abella and a nephew of Imelda Marcos.

Ten days of hectic bargaining found the MNLF panel absolutely intransigent, but Libyan leader Gaddafi was determined that the talks succeed. Deputy Minister Mike Barbero and Pex Castro met with Gaddafi three times to explain the Philippine position and ask for his support.

There were three points of contention:

o   The Philippine panel insisted that the Presidential Decree granting autonomy to Muslim Mindanao, as per the Tripoli Agreement, must be subject to a referendum/plebiscite as required by the Philippine Constitution of 1973.

o Consul Ali Taupan of the Philippine panel who controlled the Arab text, and our Ambassador Pex Castro who controlled the French text, insisted that the "Regional Security Force" required by the Agreement, should mean local police units for the maintenance of public peace and order, not an army organized for battle.

o The third contentious issue left unresolved was the title of the Agreement. The MNLF insisted that it be titled "Autonomy for Muslim Mindanao" while the Philippine panel insisted that it be "Autonomy in Southern Philippines." There was a deadlock here.

So the Tripoli Agreement had no formal title, unlike other agreements. It is the only Agreement in the world that starts with an Islamic greeting, "BISMILLAH AD RAHMAN AL RAHIM": In the name of God, the most Compassionate and Merciful...

The Tripoli Agreement was signed at three o'clock in the morning, before the dawn of December 24, 1976, although it was dated December 23.

Since the Tripoli Agreement is only a framework agreement embodying principles for regional internal autonomy, the MNLF sent a delegation to Zamboanga in Mindanao, accompanied by the OIC secretary general, and the OIC Quadripartite Committee composed of representatives from Libya, Saudi Arabia, Senegal and Somalia. With these in attendance the cease-fire agreement was signed between the Philippines and the MNLF on January 7, 1977.

The story on the MNLF, the Tripoli Agreement and the Jeddah Accords will be concluded tomorrow

Part Seven: The Jedda Accords, a new ballgame
In February 1977, the panel headed by Deputy Minister Mike Barbero -- with Ambassador Pex Castro as vice-chairman, and members Justice Minerva Reyes as legal adviser, Asst. Secretary for Local Government Ronnie Puno (brother of TV host Dong Puno), Col. Eddie Ermita and General Paciencio Magtibay -- went back to Tripoli to finalize arrangements under the Tripoli Agreement.

This time for one whole month, MNLF's Nur Misuari insisted on Secession in gross violation of the Tripoli Agreement. And because of the impasse, Marcos decided to send his wife Imelda for the second time, to reason with Libyan leader Gaddafi and urge him to pressure Misuari to adhere to the agreement and accept autonomy, not secession.

Gaddafi agreed and sent Marcos a telex on March 18th proposing that the Tripoli Agreement be implemented immediately by:

o A presidential proclamation declaring autonomy in the 13 provinces mentioned in the Agreement: Sulu, Basilan, Tawi-Tawi, Zamboanga del Norte, Zamboanga del Sur, Lanao del Norte, Lanao del Sur, Cotabato, Maguindanao, Sultan Kudarat, Palawan, South Cotabato, Davao del Sur.

o A provisional government organized to supervise the referendum.

o A presidential decree issued to set up the autonomous government.

Marcos accepted the terms by telex, and proclaimed autonomy. He offered Nur Misuari the chairmanship of the provisional government, which Misuari rejected.

In April 1977 the MNLF delegation headed by Kagim Jajurie of Sulu came, accompanied by the OIC secretary general, Foreign Minister Treki of Libya, Foreign Minister Assane Seck of Senegal, and the Quadripartite Committee. Marcos upgraded the Philippine panel to cabinet level: Foreign Minister Carlos P. Romulo as chairman, Defense Minister Juan Ponce Enrile as vice-chairman, and members Justice Minister Vicente Abad Santos, Local Government Minister Jose Roño, General Fidel Ramos, and Ambassador Pex Castro who did the French interpretation.

On April 17, 1977, Marcos proceeded with the Referendum and then created two autonomous regions, Region 9 and 12, excluding South Cotabato, Davao del Sur and Palawan which rejected autonomy during the referendum.

The autonomous Region 9 had Bob Tugung as chairman. But he was subsequently assassinated in front of Filipinas Hotel during the November 22, 1986, attempted coup. He was succeeded by his widow Elnorita Tugung, an appointee of President Cory. The Regional 9 Assemby is headed by Speaker Nur Hussein Ututalum.

The autonomous Region 12 had Simeon Datumanong as its first chairman, with Speaker Abdul Khayer Alonto heading the Regional Assembly. Datumanong became Minister for Muslim Affairs, and was succeeded as chairman by MNLF Commander Ronnie Malagiok. Alonto who ran for Senator under GAD was succeeded as Speaker by Makabankit Lanto.

Sometime in March 1982, President Marcos went on a State Visit to Saudi Arabia. His host King Khalid told him that Nur Misuari and the MNLF were fooling the OIC all along, and therefore, King Khalid said, the OIC will no longer support Misuari, provided however that Marcos implemented the Tripoli Agreement in full.

Nur Misuari then became a non-entity. But surprisingly, after the EDSA revolution, on September 5, 1986, President Cory went to Mindanao to meet Misuari. In January 1987, "Agapito Butz" Aquino and Aquilino "Nene" Pimentel went to Saudi Arabia to sign the Jeddah Accords by which the new government promised to discuss autonomy for the 23 provinces of Mindanao!

It is a new ball game. This time the Philippine panel is headed by Ambassador Emmanuel Pelaez, and the MNLF Panel by Habib Hashim. The MNLF again insisted on secession, and the talks collapsed May 7, 1987.

The new 1987 Constitution mandates Autonomy for Muslim Mindanao to be formulated by a Regional Consultative Council (RCC) which will be submitted to Congress. In March 1988, President Cory organized the RCC in Cotabato City. The RCC is to submit a draft of a bill on autonomy by September 30, 1988. And according to the Constitution, the bill must become law before December 31, 1988.

On September 16, last Friday as we mentioned in the beginning, the RCC requested an audience with President Cory to discuss the three major issues of contention, the same as in Tripoli in December, 1976.

History comes to a full circle and repeats itself. At least one character, Ambassador Pex Castro whom the Muslims called Castro the inFidel comes back from the past, for a repeat performance in the same capacity. And as before, the same contentious issues remain:

o Autonomy in Southern Philippines versus Autonomy for Muslim Mindanao.

o Regional security forces as local police units for the maintenance of public peace and order versus the Bangsamoro Army organized for defense and offense.

o The Title of the bill that would determine whether the region will be conceived as an Internal Autonomy, or a State Within a State.

Part Eight: Shahani versus her Papa on Sabah

There are actually two areas that figure in our present problem with Malaysia:

o   The Kalayaan Group of islands discovered by Tomas Cloma, west of Palawan in the South China Sea, once thought to be part of the Spratly group, and subject to conflicting and overlapping claims of China, Vietnam, Taiwan, Malaysia and the Philippines. It was here in Rizal Reef that Commodore Gil Fernandez blew up the Malaysian concrete pylon, and the three Philippine fishing boats and their 69 crew members were apprehended by the Malaysian Navy. Read Part Two and Three of this series.

o   Sulu Sea Triangle, only thirty miles off the coast of Sandakan, consisting of six islands of the Turtle Island group, which was reportedly subjected to seven intrusions by the Malaysians from January to August this year, and which was mistakenly claimed to have been annexed by Malaysia. This part of the series deals with the Sulu Sea Triangle and our claim on Sabah.

In the Treaty of Paris of 1898, marking the end of the four-month joke of a war between the United States and Spain (only about 400 Americans died), Spain sold us to the USA at $2.00 a head. They were paid $20 million for the 10 million Filipinos and their native land.

The $20 million assuaged the honor of comic opera Conquistadores who failed to fight a credible war, losing nine ships and 381 sailors against ZERO losses of the US in the Battle of Manila Bay. The only American casualty died of heat prostration shoveling coal into the furnace of Dewey's flagship SS Olympia.

The Treaty of Paris, however, did not adequately define the frontier between Borneo and Sulu. So in January 2, 1930, American and British diplomats met in Washington DC, to sign an Agreement entitled "Convention delimiting the Boundary between the Philippine Archipelago and North Borneo." This put the six islands of the Sulu Sea Triangle squarely within Philippine jurisdiction.

The Convention did not however make clear the status of the island of Taganak, which the British kept and on which they built a lighthouse, because the island was a strategic crossing point between Sabah and Sulu.

In 1947, the British formally agreed to turn over the Taganak Island and lighthouse to the Philippine Republic. President Manuel Roxas and his Vice President and Foreign Secretary Elpidio Quirino, sent a young legal officer by the name of Diosdado "Dadong" Macapagal to hoist the Philippine flag, the good ole Sun and Stars, and unveil a ceremonial plaque, after the British hauled down their Union Jack.

In official Malaysian maps the islands are shown to be under the Philippines. However in certain navigational maps distributed by the Malaysian government, it would seem that the six islands of the Sulu Sea Triangle are shown to be Malaysian Territory. This triggered a crisis when Sen. Leticia Shahani accused the Malaysians of annexing Philippine territory and demanded that our Ambassador to Malaysia be recalled at once. The Malaysians satisfactorily explained that the dotted lines represented not the boundary, but the navigational route through the islands, allowed under the doctrine of innocent passage.

Taganak was part of the Turtle Island group, so called because the island became the sanctuary of thousands of turtles. Because of his experience in negotiating for and recovering the Turtle Islands, Dadong Macapagal vowed that if and when he became President of the Republic, he would also recover Sabah for the Philippines. Sandakan in Sabah is only 30 miles from Taganak, separated by a strait narrower than the English Channel.

When Macapagal became President, he appointed his vice president Emmanuel Pelaez as Foreign Secretary. Pelaez even then was plotting to succeed Macapagal as president and was hesitant to file a claim for Sabah because it might displease the Americans and derail his presidential plans.

It fell to S.P. Lopez who subsequently succeeded Pelaez as Foreign Secretary, to draft the *Note Verbale* for the Sabah Claim and route it to the British Ambassador Sir John Pilcher. Sir John, one remembers vividly, had a very beautiful daughter named Ann who was the subject of amorous pursuit by every eligible bachelor and dirty old man (DOM) in Manila. Even with such maddening distraction, Sir John managed to convey the message to London, that "the little brown monkeys" were beginning to assert themselves, and therefore the time has come to do something about North Borneo which was transferred from the jurisdiction of the North Borneo Company to the British crown when the Philippines regained its independence from Mommie Dearest America in 1946.

It was then that Britain decided to create a new nation called Malaysia to include the disputed Sabah. The British capacity to divide-and-conquer and create mischief, is of course legendary, and is responsible for most of the misery in this world. The story of our long and frustrating struggle to recover our lost territory does not belong here. It was summarized in our Make Our Day columns of Aug. 31 and Sept. 3, and will be told in great detail in another series of articles.

Suffice to mention that the Philippines broke off relations with Malaysia twice before:

o First was on August 30, 1963, when President Diosdado Macapagal of the Philippines and President Sukarno of Indonesia refused to recognize the new state of Malaysia, and withdrew their embassies from Kuala Lumpur, capital of the old Union of Malaya.

o Second was on October 15, 1968, when then Secretary of Foreign Affairs Narciso Ramos, the late father of Senator Leticia Ramos Shahani and Defense Secretary Fidel V. Ramos, declared in a speech before the 23rd UN Assembly, that until the Sabah claim is settled, "the Philippine Government cannot and does not recognize the powers, competence or authority of the Government of Malaysia to represent or speak for the people of the Territory of Sabah..."

It would seem that the views of the elder statesman Narciso Ramos conflict with those of his daughter Senator Letty Shahani, who introduce an administration bill in the Senate officially dropping the Philippine claim to Sabah, a bill placed in suspended animation during the recent crisis in our Malaysian relations, and we hope, consigned permanently to the ashcan.

Senator Shahani also introduced a senate resolution that mandates a clear, consistent and unequivocal foreign policy based on National Interest, and not on the dictates of Foggy Bottom in Washington DC. -- a step that is long long overdue.

Part Nine: Conclusion -- How do we achieve a credible foreign policy?

After reading the earthshaking foreign policy statements of our leaders -- legislators, executive officials, newspaper columnists and editorial writers -- calculated to grab headlines and sell papers, one agonizes at the realization that they are totally ignorant of the most vital point of international relations, which is that nations, like people, play games. And that to play the game well, we must not only know the rules of the game, but must also train a group of players to play as a team. Further, we must not only achieve winning scores, but better still, display skills and maneuvers to outplay our adversaries and win the admiration of the spectators.

We must remember that although we are the first to regain our independence from western imperialism on July 4, 1946, we are in a region of ancient nations which are not only demographic giants but veterans in the diplomatic game.

o In China, the oldest surviving civilization, the legendary Emperor Yao of China received envoys from neighboring tribes as early as 2353 BC.

o In ancient India, the Laws of Manu decreed that only "worthy men" be named envoys to neighboring nations.

o Egypt's Rameses II signed an offensive and defensive alliance with the Hittites in 1280 BC.

o The Japanese Shoguns had a long history of relations with ancient Korea and China.

o The Chakri dynasty of Thailand which is 200 years old, was able to fend off the imperialist powers by astute diplomacy.

Our neighbors are not only diplomatic veterans, they have since refined the rules of the games nations play. Apparently our leaders have yet to know what these games are.

FIRST and foremost, anybody dabbling in diplomacy, diplomat or government leader or newspaper columnist, should go to the nearest bookstore and buy the book "Games Nations Play: Analyzing International Politics" by Professor John Spanier, now on its fourth edition, considered the Bible of diplomacy. Since it is only 589 pages, reasonably educated politicians and newspaper pundits should be able to browse through it, or even finish reading it over the weekend, if they forego watching the boob tube, of course.

Having realized that we are indeed infants in the diplomatic game, we must now overcome our naiveté by allowing our professional diplomats who must have read the book, or at least seen copies of it at the second-hand book depot of Barnes & Nobles, in front of St. Patrick's Cathedral in New York City, unhampered study of our major diplomatic problems. At least our politicians should read professional reports by diplomats before taking the floor in Congress for a sophomoric discourse on diplomacy.

SECOND, our educated leaders should endeavor to meet more of the foreign ambassadors, at least 52 of them living in North Forbes, South Forbes and Dasmariñas Villages -- and not leave the poor diplomats to the tender mercies of empty-headed society matrons and their boorish husbands whose main topic of conversation is the shopping they do in New York and Paris.

On the other hand, the foreign ambassadors should not limit their contacts to the old rich and *noveau riche* of the villages, some of whom are really decadent and colonial-minded, but endeavor to meet the decision makers and opinion makers of the nation, especially politicians, journalists, professors, student leaders, and known nationalists.

THIRD, we must have young professionals in diplomatic service.

The first thing one notices about foreign ambassadors is that most of them are young, in their early forties or fifties, hardly anybody in his sixties. Even China and Japan which used to send old doddering ambassadors to Manila, are now represented by young ambassadors in their early middle age. Ambassadors from ASEAN countries except the Philippines, are retired and sent to pasture by the time they are 55 years of age, at most.

The second thing one notices is that most, if not all, these foreign ambassadors are professionals, experienced diplomats with at least 20 years of varied posting in different regions of the world, which give them a mature and sophisticated view of geopolitics.

In sharp contrast, we in the Philippines persist in the obsolete practice, long discarded by all nations, young or old, of sending out as envoys, retired politicians, officials and businessmen who are not only old men, but are unschooled in the art of diplomacy.

Rags and Riches

Most of the diplomats assigned to important posts are retired old men, who are mostly amateurs in the diplomatic game, mostly in their 70s: Ramon del Rosario (Tokyo), Emmanuel Pelaez (Washington), Nicanor Jimenez, Jose Ingles, Salvador P. Lopez (who is a bit deaf), Jorge Coquia (asst. sec. for legal affairs), Israel Bocobo (asst. sec. for labor), Col. Faustino David (asst. sec. for intelligence), Abdul Gaffar Alonto (to Libya), the retired Chief Justice Claudio Teehankee (to the United Nations).

FOURTH, we must train them to be good diplomats.

Most nations give rigorous and specialized training to young professionals in foreign service: Foreign Service Institute in McLean, Virginia; Ecole Nationale d'Administration (ENA) in Paris; Foreign Service Institute outside of Bonn; Escuela Diplomatica in Madrid; Institut Universitaire des Hautes Etudes Internationale de Geneve in Switzerland; Vienna School of Diplomacy that produced Metternich the mastermind of the Congress of Vienna.

Our first diplomats in 1946-47 were sent to the Foreign Service Institute in the USA for a six weeks crash course. They were 25 young men, among them Jose Alejandrino, Delfin Garcia, Luis Moreno Salcedo, Carlos Faustino, Hortencio Brillantes, etc., now all retired.

Today's professional diplomats were of the second generation, nurtured under the wing of the young and boyish idealist Raul S. Manglapus, undersecretary of Foreign Affairs, way back in 1956-57: Ambassadors Virgilio Nañagas (Columbia U. topnotcher, to San Francisco), Pablo Araque (from Vienna School of Diplomacy, to India), Pablo Suarez (Columbia U., to Kuala Lumpur), Sergio Barrera (UST, to Canada), Tomas Padilla (Yale, to Korea), Pacifico Castro (Institut Universitaire des Hautes Etudes Internationale de Geneve, now Director General of Arab and African Affairs); Rodolfo Sanchez (Columbia U., now detailed to Salonga), Ernesto Pineda (formerly to New York, fired for defending Marcos).

The diplomatic game today is not for old men good at delivering motherhood speeches, hosting dinners and enjoying the perquisites of a dollar-denominated income and tax-free importation -- but dynamic young professionals on the go, specially trained to promote, protect and defend our national interest.

The sad spectacle of the Philippine diplomatic service today is that 25 of our 52 Embassies and Missions in the most important capitals, are occupied by unprofessional political appointees rewarded for service to the EDSA revolution. Our career ambassadors are sent only to such exotic posts as Lagos, Nairobi, Libreville, Santiago, Lima, etc. while the amateur geriatrics are just living it up in the watering holes of the world.

The result is that we have progressively declining terms of trade with the European Economic Community and just about all other industrial nations. There is bad publicity because our envoys do not bother to defend the Cory Government. They telex *verbatim* the bad articles and ask the department to send the replies, since most of our political envoys can not write good English!

We have never assigned a professional ambassador in Tokyo, Washington DC or Madrid during the Marcos years, and even now we continue to relegate our professional envoys to the back waters of the world.

I repeat, since nations like people play games, only those who know the rules of the game and have played it before, can be counted upon to carry the ball game for us. We should now assign professional diplomats to Tokyo, Washington DC, London, Bonn, Madrid, Riyadh -- and probably then we can have a diplomatic service really to be proud of.

FIFTH, our diplomatic service must be run by the office constitutionally charged with the responsibility, the Foreign Affairs department.

The foreign offices or ministries of all our competitors in the diplomatic game are run by professionals. But what do we have in the Philippines? During the Marcos dictatorship, foreign policy was handled by a clique in Aguado street, next door to Cory's residence today, which was operated by Ambassador Kokoy Romualdez and his side-kick, Ambassador Rafael Gonzales (now in East Berlin), brother-in-law of Health Secretary Alran Bengzon and husband of Ambassador Felicidad Bengzon Gonzales in Paris.

The Aguado was the real foreign office during the Marcos years. The ambassadors of great powers like Ambassadors Armacost and Bosworth (USA), Sumiya (Japan), Sholmov (USSR), Chen (China), Shobokshi (Saudi Arabia) and McLaren

(Great Britain) only dealt with Aguado and snubbed Padre Faura. This made the Foreign Ministers, both General Carlos P. Romulo and his successor the feisty Arturo Tolentino, denounced privately with Marcos and publicly in the press, Kokoy's Aguado office.

But Aguado remained and exercised real diplomatic power up to the bitter end. In fact, Aguado conducted the 1983 RP-US military bases review without informing Padre Faura of the developments. Surprisingly, Aguado diehards like Ambassador Ralph Gonzales, a karate blackbelter, and Ambassador Leonie Caday who was Kokoy's shadow and voice in the 1983 bases talks, are still dramatis personae today. While Aguado has been physically dismantled, it may still exist in a new form. The new "Aguado" today is said to exist in the form of the 30 "Special Assistants" and six "Assistant Secretaries" who are being accused of forming a cordon sanitaire around Manglapus and of shunting aside all the professionals who head the different offices in Foreign office.

In the highest national interest, Manglapus should now meet with the career officers every so often in Puerto Azul or Tagaytay, as Romulo used to do, for a free wheeling discussion of issues and problems of the department. He may be surprised to find out that the professionals have something important to contribute to the national good, as propounded in the book "Modern Ambassador" by Martin F. Herz from Raul's alma mater, Georgetown University in Washington D.C. We should now begin anew by harnessing all available experienced talent in Foreign department.

After having resolved the basic problems of experienced manpower, resource utilization and genuine national reconciliation in foreign relations, there is no reason why we cannot chart a better and more honorable posture in our diplomacy instead of the amateurish actions of politicians who may yet bring us not only dishonor but tragedy of untold proportions.

We have 987 treaties and international agreements concluded with more than 100 countries and neatly printed in 9 thick volumes of the Philippine Treaty Series of the UP Law Center and Foreign Department.

Let us now buckle down to work. It is a difficult and laborious process to go over and analyze the 987 treaties, discard the erroneous agreements if any, and negotiate and conclude new ones to protect and advance our national interest.

But we can only do these backbreaking tasks if we immediately retire all those in the foreign service above 65 years old, especially the deaf and the physically handicapped. Let us trust and support all our professional trained diplomats because we have not only spent good money for their training but invested much in their experience.

Foreign policies are not made overnight, and diplomats, good serious mature diplomats, cannot be brewed instantly like coffee or tea!

September 9-21,1988

ooooo

MUSLIMS and MALAYSIA

1. Muslims may revolt to embarrass us during the APEC meeting

Let's face it. We are facing a national crisis similar to what happened in Croatia and in the Soviet Union during recent years, and periodically in India. And we only hope it will not result in bloody ethnic cleansing of gargantuan and ungovernable proportions.

Let's face it. Muslim leaders want their own political domain, under their political and economic control, and that does not mean the empowerment of the common Muslim citizens in their area, for feudalism and warlordism is more endemic and much more rampant in Muslim society than anywhere else in the Philippines. There are personal fortunes to be made when and if they get direct aid and economic support from the rich countries of the Middle East.

To achieve this they are willing to take up arms and launch holy war, or *jihad*, for only then can they can get full and exclusive support of the Arab states, Malaysia and our powerful neighbor Indonesia. The reason Muslim leaders insist on keeping their arms and constantly making threats of war is because the Muslim Koran sanctions holy war against "unbelievers." Once the other Muslim countries are made to believe this, they are under religious obligation to make war on the neighboring non-Muslims.

That is why our government is gingerly treading on dangerous grounds, bending backward to keep the peace, even as ex-Senator Tolentino is accusing it of surrendering to the Muslims. There is a window of opportunity for Muslim leaders to focus international attention on their situation, and try to get the sympathy of other Muslim nations. That window of opportunity may come during the coming APEC conference in the next few months -- where the United States and Japan are seeking to secure their economic hegemony over our part of the world. One may expect a series of military actions and acts of terrorism to embarrass the Philippines in this our moment of weakness.

Anding Roces quotes the book Islam by Henry Masse; "What are the Rules of Holy War? It was obligatory to fight against the people of the neighboring non-Muslim territories of Islam. That is to say, the territories of war *(dar-al-harb)* must be transferred into territories of Islam *(dar-al-Islam).* Between these two extremes came the tributary lands conquered by peaceful means, that is by treaty *(daras-Suhl).* This third category became subject first to persuasive methods."

The third category is exactly what the Tripoli Agreement is all about. The Tripoli Agreement was signed by the late dictator Ferdinand Marcos on December 23, 1979, brokered by his wife Imelda in response to a need to accommodate the Arab nations at the time we needed their oil. It was a sordid deal that placed our sovereign nation under the supervision of the Organization of Islamic Conference, originally founded by reactionary fundamentalist Arab states to counter socialist ideas. And there is no doubt that Marcos intended to temporarily mollify the Muslims until he can double-cross them with impunity.

The Muslims on the other hand are not above violating the terms of any treaty if there is an opportunity to advance to their ultimate goal, complete separation and independence from their Christian brothers.

2. It is folly to think the Muslims are part of our nation
What the Muslims aim for is no less than absolute and total independence, or at least a separate and autonomous nation within our state, even it means total war. From the inception of colonial rule, Spain engaged the Muslims in continuous warfare. In 1876 the Spaniards concluded a treaty with the Sultan of Sulu in which the latter recognized the sovereignty of Spain for an annual pension for the Sultan and his heirs. The treaty was more honored in the breach than in the observance of its provisions. Then, as now, the Muslims secured temporary truce until they were strong enough to continue their war. The war continued during the early part of the American Occupation, continues even today against the forces of our republic. The Muslims continue to regard themselves as a separate nation.

One should never confuse "state" with "nation." A nation is a people bound together by race, religion, language, culture or historical experience. A state is a people governed by one government. The two do not necessarily coincide, nor are they mutually exclusive. Quebec is a French-speaking nation within the state of Canada. Belgium is divided into the French-speaking Walloons and the Dutch-speaking Flemish. Yugoslavia is divided between Muslims and Christians, Serbs and Croats, all at war with each other. Great Britain is made up of the English, the Welsh, the Scots and Irish. The Spaniards speak different languages: Castillan (which we call Spanish), Catalans (Barcelona), and the Basques who want their independence.

In the Philippines, most tribes (Ilocanos, Tagalogs, Bicolanos, Cebuanos, Ilonggos) are bound together by religion and a common historical experience, most of all, by integration through intermarriage, ease of migration, fraternization and urbanization. The Muslims of the south stand apart because of differences in religion and culture. Left behind by the march of economic progress, most of them have not traveled more than 25 kilometers from where they born. And they face a traumatic cultural clash every time they meet Christians.

These Muslims were collectively known to Spaniards are Moros or Moors, in memory of the Muslim Arabs of Morocco who occupied southern Spain for 800 years. But they are divided into tribes often antagonistic to each other. Still with the cohesion of Islam they were the best organized force to resist the Spanish invaders. They were never really conquered by Spain, otherwise the Philippines of today would have had a much larger territory extending all the way to Borneo.

The Muslims have never been comfortable being called Filipinos -- after the most Christian King Philip II of Spain. They have never been comfortable with our laws derived from the Roman Law or Napoleonic Code from Spain. For their customs, laws and practices, they look to their co-religionists among the Arabs, and it is to Mecca and Cairo that they go for education, religious guidance, and pilgrimages.

In the strictest sense, Muslims are a separate nation unto themselves. And it is folly on our part even to think of integrating them fully into our body politic, any more than the Muslims in India and in Croatia can achieve more than a precarious peace with their Hindu and Christian compatriots.
July 15-16, 1996, ISYU

3. Because of the Muslims we lost Sabah

It is an extreme irony of history that we honor the Muslims of the South for having successfully resisted the Spanish conquistadores in Borneo, when we who are now Christians succumbed to the friars and Spain and took three and a half centuries to cast off the yoke of Western colonialism. For years our leaders have been proposing that in recognition of Muslim resistance, we put a 9th ray among the 8 rays of the sun on our flag in memory of first eight provinces who rose up against Spain in 1898.

Yet we bemoan the loss of Sabah in Borneo which could have been a part of the Philippines had the Spaniards were able to beat the Muslims in the early days. The Muslims were triumphant because their fierce and intrepid warriors had a psychological impact on Christian Spaniards, who themselves were invaded by the Muslim Moors of Morocco from the coast of North Africa, crossing the Mediterranean and occupying Spain for 800 years. Think of it, Spain occupied the Philippines for barely 350 years, but Spain was occupied by the Moors for 800 years.

That is why the Spanish word for Moor, "Moro," is applied to our Muslim brothers in the South. And that is why the Spaniards were psychologically unprepared to deal decisively with our Moros. If they were then Spain would have occupied Sabah as well, and our country might have been 25 percent larger than it actually is., and a lot richer too because Sabah now produces oil and has a lot of oil reserves.

British agents with a measly sum of 5,000 Singapore dollars a year, conned the Sultan of Sulu in the 1878, into giving them a ``perpetual lease" on Sabah. When we tried to get it back, the British North Borneo Co. that owned it, transferred it to the jurisdiction of the British crown in 1946 (only 11 days before our independence). The British then transferred it in 1963 just after we filed a claimon June 22, 1962) to the hastily created state of Malaysia.

When we pressed our claim peacefully, Great Britain and Australia mobilized their troops in Singapore to confront us, while the Americans told us that if their British and Australian cousins attack us, we cannot rely on Americans to help us under our mutual defense treaty. The treaty, the Americans told us, is only directed against America's enemies, not ours.

We asked to have our Sabah claim adjudicated by the World Court at The Hague. Malaysian leader Tunko Abdul Rahman as quoted by President Macapagal, agreed but the asshole Britishers "insisted" that he stonewall the claim. So we should not really

rejoice that our Muslims were fierce enough to resist Spain.
Said Macapagal in his memoirs A Stone for the Edifice (page 289):
``Unless Sabah become an independent state by itself, it shall be
the continuing duty of our posterity to carry on the endeavor to
return Sabah to the Philippines."
September 27, 1995, ISYU

4. Malaysia conspired to create the MNLF

IN 1969, Tunku Abdul Rahman, Prime Minister of Malaysia,
cooked up a fantastic conspiracy against the Philippines. He
invited Filipino Muslim leaders Nur Misuari, Hashim Salamat, Sali
Wali and 90 young fighters to Kota Kinabalu, capital of Sabah.
From there they were airlifted, accompanied by Malaysian
officers, to the island of Pulau Pangkor, trained, fully armed, and
with the help of Raschid Lucman brought back to Mindanao to
start the Moro National Liberation Movement (MNLF).

Why? Because the Tunku wanted revenge for our filing a
claim for Sabah in 1963. When Tunku Abdul Rahman ceased to
be Prime Minister, he maneuvered to get himself elected as the
First Secretary General of the Organization of Islamic Conference
(OIC), and as such, in 1972, he inscribed a separate agenda item
on the MNLF in the OIC. Today the Tunku still lives and works like
me, as a columnist of the Malaysian Star. As long as he lives, no
one dares take off the MNLF agenda in the OIC, which continues
to be a thorn in our side.

In 1977, just before Marcos attended the 2nd Summit at
Kuala Lumpur, he was given a 250-page document, "The Sabah
Affair'-- which described the entire saga of the Philippine claim to
Sabah. This document details how we lost three opportunities to
bring our claim to the World Court, and win it, despite the fact that
all parties must agree to accept the verdict of the Court.

o The first opportunity came in 1948 when our Foreign
Undersecretary Bernabe Africa sent a note to the British Legation
in Manila to collect the rentals promised to the Sultan of Sulu. At
the time the British could not have resisted a unilateral demand
from the Philippines to settle the Sabah claim in the World Court,
because in the same year the British unilaterally sued Albania in
the World Court on the Corfu Channel Case where a British ship
was sunk by Albanian mines.

The British developed the theory of *"forum prorogatum"* for extending the court's jurisdiction, which the Philippines at the time could have used to bring the matter of Sabah into the jurisdiction of the World Court. But we did not. Damn!

o The second opportunity came in March 1963, after the London Talks with Vice President and Foreign Secretary Emmanuel Pelaez as chairman, SP Lopez as vice-chairman, and Jovito Salonga and Totoy Feliciano in the legal panel. The British agreed to exchange documents with us on the Sabah claim. Yet when they came to Manila to do so, for some unexplained reason, we got cold feet and refused to go through with it! Damn!

Lela Noble, author of a book on the Sabah claim published by University of Arizona, could not understand why the Philippines backed out of the exchange of documents. If we brought it to the World Court, we could have won our case.

o The third opportunity came with the "UN Ascertainment Mission'" to determine the wishes of the Sabah population. From the very beginning, the British maneuvered to have only white men in favor of Malaysia to compose the Mission; and the Malaysian government put all sorts of obstacles to Filipino observers there. When in October 1963, the Mission reported to the UN General Assembly that majority of Sabahans would rather join Malaysia -- both Indonesia and the Philippines objected. And this would have been sufficient cause to go to the World Court to get an "advisory judgment." But Foreign Secretary SP Lopez did not pursue the case. Damn!

What we are not told is that during the London talks, the British Foreign Minister Lord Homes told our Foreign Secretary Pelaez, "If you touch Sabah, you'll get a bloody nose!" And Pelaez got scared shit.

The Australians, damn them, sent their only aircraft carrier, the hand-me-down HMS Hermes (not Herpes) to our Balabak Straits south of Palawan, and to our Sibutu Passage near Tawi-Tawi, and rushed two squadrons of their Mirage fighter bombers to Fort Butterworth in Malaysia.

President Lyndon Johnson sent the Attorney General Robert Kennedy, to tell our President Macapagal not to touch North Borneo, because the USA will back up the British and Australians if they went to war with the Philippines, despite of our Mutual Defense Treaty. Americans be damned!

The UN Secretary General U Thant, a Burmese, begged SP Lopez, "I am the first Asian to be head of UN, please do not embarrass me!" And Lopez acquiesced! Damn!

We had three chances to bring our Sabah claim to the World Court, and we could have won peacefully! Unfortunately we Filipinos did not have the sense of nationalism and political will to discern and to struggle for our national interest. Dung.
August 3, 1988

5. We kowtow even to Malaysia; Campillo must go

THE trouble with kowtowing to Americans is that we lose our dignity, our sense of self worth, our backbone. As a result we kowtow to everyone else, including Malaysians.

By genuflecting every time we meet an American -- even the merest beachcomber, a week unwashed -- our pants wear out, our knees acquire callouses, our eyes droop to avoid the steady gaze of prideful men.

The way we handle the Sabah claim is symptomatic of the masochistic self-flagellation that characterizes our government actuations.

That we have a legitimate claim, there is no doubt. British agents with a measly sum of 5,000 Singapore dollars a year, conned the Sultan of Sulu into giving them a "perpetual lease" on Sabah. When we tried to get it back, the British North Borneo Co. that owned it, transferred it to the jurisdiction of the British crown, which then transferred it to the hastily created state of Malaysia.

When we pressed our claim peacefully, Great Britain and Australia mobilized their troops to confront us, while the Americans told us that if their British and Australian cousins attack us, we cannot rely on Americans to help us under our mutual defense treaty. The treaty, the Americans told us, is only directed against America's enemies, not ours.

We asked to have our Sabah claim adjudicated by the World Court at The Hague, but Malaysia backed up by Britain refused to have the matter settled in a peaceful, rational and civilized manner. Instead, Malaysia threatened to sever relations with us, but did not, because it is very much in its interest to join the ASEAN.

Now we are asked to drop the Sabah claim so that the Malaysian prime minister will deign to attend our Manila summit meeting, and assume a friendlier attitude.

We have no quarrel with our brother Malays, our beef is with those British dung-heaps who made us one of the many victims in their century of colonial plunder. Malaysia just happens to be the serendipitous beneficiary of British duplicity.

And all we want is a peaceful settlement of an ancient historic claim, not unlike that of Israel in the Middle East.

Why then do we kowtow to Malaysia and drop our legitimate claim? To have "friendly relations" with them? That's dung, we are the aggrieved party. We are a bigger nation, 56 million in population against their 15 million, with a higher literacy rate, a more homogeneous population (they are 38 percent Chinese).

Frankly, they should worry about our friendship more than we should theirs. But our colonial mentality, our constant kowtowing to foreigners have emboldened them, with the advice of Britishers, to try to bully and bamboozle us.

Why cannot our government protect the rights of our citizens the Sultanate of Sulu, and those of our own nation? Why do we give way to the Americans on the bases, to Belgian Ambassador Alain Rens now back and raring to fire more Filipinos in his staff, to a mere military attache Victor Raphael who blatantly backed rebel forces, to the Japanese, Singaporeans, Malaysians?

They all treat us like dung. And we deserve it.

Come on Cory, Raul, let the Sabah resolution die unresolved in the Senate. Keep the claim in the freezer if need be, but keep it alive to show posterity that our generation, despite worn out pants and calloused knees, has at least some shred of dignity left to redress a historic grievance.

But first let us get rid of the Gunga Dins in our midst, like Sostenes Campillo, alleged gun-runner, airport expediter of Kaplan's baggage, world class tourist who visits his daughter at government expense, godfather of foreign guides, promoter of foreign domination of Filipino tourist agencies.

We are talking about Sostenes Campillo Junior, not Sostenes Senior who was the friend of Madame X, not Lito his brother who shot dead a BIR man in Shellbourne Hotel, nor

Sostenes the Third who is allegedly employed in a Tourism agency.

We are talking of Tourism undersecretary Sostenes Campillo Jr., husband of Tessie Galvez (daughter of PAL pilot Eugenio Galvez) who is a charming wonderful woman.

But Sostenes is something else. He is so anti-Filipino that the Tourist Guides and the Tourist Agencies want him out.

He is about to issue new regulations governing the use of foreign tourist guides in the Philippines. It is bad enough that he now allows two foreign guides per agency; soon he wants to allow two foreign guides per nationality per agency. Theoretically each tourist agency may hire two Japanese, two Koreans, two Chinese, two French, two Germans *ad nauseum*.

What the Filipino Guides, many of them professors and retired Foreign Affairs personnel, rightfully demand is that the tourist guides be our own citizens, with rare exceptions, as foreigners practice in their own countries.

Even the Tour Agencies are demanding the ouster of Sostenes. Ermin Garcia Jr., president of the Philippine Travel Agencies Association (PTAA) accuses Sostenes of conspiring against an organization representing 92 percent of the total number of licensed agencies, by promoting the proliferation of other organizations, and by favoring foreign-based IATA Agents Travel Association (PIATA) which he himself founded.

Sostenes does this to destroy the unity and effectiveness of Filipino agencies, accrediting the PIATA for inclusion in the Philippine Agency Program Joint Council; proposing a "multi-license" scheme aimed at the disbandment of PTAA; encouraging PIATA, PHILTOA, and NITAS to take different positions on DOT matters; and keeping several TCP members from dialoguing with Secretary Gonzalez.

Sostenes fired employes Amelia Zuniga, Hortencia E. Lasin, Emma Jasmin, Virginia Nayve, Archie Vargas, Eduardo Arnaldo, Apromiano Sabordo, to replace them with his own, without the decency to pay them their separation pay, while traveling and visiting his daughter at government expense.

Campillo must go.

December 10, 1987

6. Malaysian agents burned our Foreign Office

My compadre and former boss, ex-president Diosdado Macapagal sent me a note, correcting my statement that President John Kennedy sent his brother Robert to President Macapagal not to touch Borneo.

Macapagal said it was not President Kennedy (who was assassinated the previous year) but President Lyndon Johnson who sent Robert Kennedy here in January 1964 to elicit his support for a "ceasefire in the worsening Indonesian-Malaysia hostilities in Sarawak and Sabah after the Manila Summit on August 25, 1963."

The American government under President Kennedy officially opposed our Sabah claim in writing. Macapagal filed the claim anyway on June 22, 1962. But neither the British or the Malaysians were agreeable to accept the jurisdiction of the World Court over the Sabah claim.

On the telephone, my compadre Cong Dadong Macapagal, who now writes a Sunday column in the Bulletin, said that the relations between him and Tunku Abdul Rahman were friendly. The Tunku admitted to Cong Dadong that he did not want Sabah, having enough trouble in Malaysia itself, but "the British insisted."

According to Macapagal's notes, he and the Tunku "agreed in principle to settle the claim through the World Court but lacked the time to work out the process during my term which ended in 1965." Only with the ascendancy of Marcos did the relations between Malaysia and the Philippines deteriorate.

Said Macapagal in his memoirs A Stone for the Edifice (page 289): "Unless Sabah become an independent state by itself, it shall be the continuing duty of our posterity to carry on the endeavor to return Sabah to the Philippines."

There is no inconsistency in maintaining friendly relations with Malaysia and pursuing the claim peacefully. After all, Gibraltar is still being claimed by Spain from the British, the Kuriles by Japanese from Soviet Union, and there are still disputed territories in the border between China and Russia.

Diosdado Macapagal became interested in the Sabah claim when as an official in the Foreign Affairs, he was told by Vice-President and Foreign Secretary Elpidio Quirino to negotiate for the return of Turtle Islands 18 miles off the coast Sandakan in Sept. 5, 1947.

"Remember you are dealing with the British," said Quirino, recalling that as Veep and Foreign Secretary, he went to London to negotiate a Treaty of Friendship and was told to take it up with a minor functionary in No. 10 Downing Street. Quirino refused to be humiliated.

Minister G.L. Gray of Sandakan wanted to chair the conference as per instructions of London, but Cong Dadong insisted that both of them act as co-chairmen to "reflect the sovereign equality of both our nations. We are no longer a colony, you know." Gray acquiesced.

On Oct. 2, 1947, Macapagal raised our flag over Turtle Islands. Since the Turtle Islands was part of the Sabah territory donated by Brunei to the Sultan of Sulu, Cong Dadong consulted an expert on Anglo-Saxon law in George Washington University who told him that the Philippines had a valid claim on Sabah.

So when Cong Dadong became Congressman, Rep. Godofredo Ramos of Aklan, Arturo Tolentino and he authored a congressional resolution supporting the Sabah Claim.
In December 1986, a fire gutted our Foreign Office, including the office of Undersecretary Mamintal Tamano who studying the Sabah claim. Most documents on the Sabah claim went up in smoke. Officially a stove was blamed for the fire.

But it is suspected that the fire was started by British and Malaysian secret agents. Our Intelligence Service Armed Forces of the Philippines (ISAFP) and the NICA did not even anticipate or react, because being adjuncts of CIA, they were interested only in spying and persecuting those who oppose American bases, multinational monopolies, and IMF policy to keep us forever agricultural.

Receiving nasty letters from Ahmad Sanusi Hashim of Malaysia, forces us to look closer into our relations with this nation of rectal dehiscences where people of the Malay race, our bloodbrothers, are treated like scum by the British, the Chinese, and Malay leaders with royal pretensions.

Tun Mustapha, the first Chief Minister of Sabah did not even want to join Malaysia. In his time, he forbade Malaysian Chinese from going to Sabah, a violation of the principle of free travel by citizens within their own country.

Mustapha, believe it or not, was born in Sulu and is a Tausog. He looked upon Sabah as his personal fiefdom, and

even entertained thoughts of joining Sabah and Mindanao into one nation for the Muslims. Wowie.
September 3, 1988

7. Malaysia, lapdog of British Imperialism

Bakit tayo nagmakaaway sa mga puñeteros dian sa Malaysia? Putang ina, Malaysia has 15.8 million population, we have 58 million. They are a mutually antagonistic racial mix: 59 percent Malay, mostly poor; 32 percent Chinese who culturally apart, economically dominant, politically repressed; and 12 percent Indian, restive and miserable -- with the British practically calling the shots. Our population is homogeneous, the Chinese barely five percent and effectively absorbed. Why do we kowtow to these constipated assholes, these pompous pipsqueaks who imprisoned 49 of our countrymen for four months since April, and now have the effrontery to warn us to stay off their fishing grounds or else?

I had a Malaysian friend, a fellow radio amateur Tunku Mohammad Archibald (callsign 9M2AT), now deceased, who once demonstrated to his Filipino friends how *bumiputras* should be treated, by beating up one to a bloody pulp. I thought he was a bit off. But I was wrong. It seems to be a national trait for Malaysian leaders to be lunatics. One made a sport of driving a Rolls Royce while shooting at the natives.

The Malaysian Prime Minister Datuk Seri Mahathir Mohammad has such a bad temper, it is told, that when he lost a golf game once, he beat his caddy to death with golf club. He is the one responsible for jailing Filipinos and treating them so shabbily that one died of heart attack.

These bastards treat us like their own low-class scum and we let them do it, instead of kicking their butts and balls. All because they are lapdogs of the British and the Australians who are the cousins of our masters the Americans. Fie, fie on them!

When in 1963, the Philippines was pressing its claim for Sabah, requesting that the matter be settled in the World Court, the British and the Australians went on a general mobilization of their armed forces with a threat to go to war against the Philippines. The US handed us a note saying that notwithstanding our Mutual Defense Treaty, the US will not defend the Philippines in case the British and Aussies declared war on us. That is our fair-weather, fine-feathered chicken of a friend, the USA, who wants our bases to fight its enemies but not ours. Fie, fie on them!

Early in the 17th century, the sultan of Sulu acquired sovereignty over Sabah as a reward for helping the sultan of Brunei suppress a rebellion. In 1878, the sultan of Sulu leased Sabah to Gustavus von Overbeck and Alfred Kent for an annual rent of 5,000 Malayan dollars.

The British North Borneo Company, not the British government, administered Sabah from 1878 to 1946; the Company in 1903 "expressly recognized that the Sultan of Sulu was sovereign in Sabah"; and when Spain and Netherlands raised objections years before, Lord Granville and the Marquis of Salisbury, Foreign Ministers of Great Britain in their time, explained that "the British government assumed no dominion or sovereign rights in Borneo which was occupied by the Company."

Eleven days after the Philippines became independent in 1946 and in a position to reclaim Sabah, the Company handed over Sabah to the British government. And when we raised the issue of Colonialism in 1963, the British handed Sabah over to the newly created nation of Malaysia.

Malaysia came into being because of the Sabah dispute, on Sept. 16, 1963, as a federation of Malaya, Singapore, Sarawak and Sabah. In 1965, Singapore left the Federation, disgusted at the way Malaysia treated its Chinese who then comprised 39 percent of the population (with Malays 48 percent and Indians 12 percent).

In the late 1960s, frustrated at the intransigence of Malaysia and Great Britain in refusing to submit the dispute to the World Court at The Hague, President Marcos plotted to invade Sabah with 'Jabidah' forces being trained in Corregidor. This monstrous plot was discovered when Ninoy Aquino exposed the massacre of Muslim soldiers by forces under Col. Eddie Martelino (alias Abdul Latif).

If we decide to drop the Sabah claim, it is to make friends, not to disown the rightness of our claim. These Malaysians, these pompous assholes who have acquired the arrogance of their British masters, now try to push us around, with the probable encouragement of the CIA as part of a plan to destabilize the Cory government.

What they need is a real good kick in the balls.

August 16, 1988

8. Recognizing The Legitimacy Of The Sultanate Of Sulu

WHEREAS, there is need for the Philippine government to deal with an entity to represent all citizens of Islamic Faith, including the armed warriors of the Maranao and Tausog tribes, as well as those of Maguindanaos, Sama, Yakan, Sangil, Badjao, Kalibugan, Jama Mapun, Iranun, Kalagan, Palawani, Molbog, as well as Christian settlers and other stakeholders – as mandatory participants without veto powers in any agreement that may resolve the Muslim problem in the Philippines;

WHEREAS, the Sultanate of Sulu and North Borneo has been a unifying authority in this part of the world since the 15th century, and continues to exist under the 33rd Sultan in a direct and unbroken line from the first Sultan, presently exercising influence by tradition, through its legitimacy and honorary position, without holding political power or sovereignty, to contribute peacefully to general good of Filipino Muslims;

WHEREAS, the Sultanate of Sulu and North Borneo was formally established in 1401 AD, with Al Sultan Shariful Hashim (a direct descendant of the Holy Prophet Mohammad) as the first Sultan of Sulu;

WHEREAS, the Sultanate gradually became the Center of Islamic influence in the Malayan region, with sovereign power and territories extending from Mindanao to the Sulu Archipelago, northwest to the entire Palawan Archipelago, Basilan, Sulu, Tawi-tawi and Sabah (North Borneo);

WHEREAS, historical diplomatic, trade and commercial ties between China and the Sultanate of Sulu existed since the Ming Dynasty (from 15th century until 1898 A.D.);

WHEREAS, the East King of Sulu (Sultan Paduka Batara) visited Ming Emperor Yongle (Zhu Di) in 1417 A.D., and died in China, leaving two sons who were raised by Chinese Muslims;

WHEREAS the Chinese Emperor built him a magnificent tomb in Dezhou District, Shandong Province, which exists to this day, and which has been declared a National Heritage Site by the Chinese authorities;

WHEREAS, the two sons of Sultan Paduka Batara stayed in China and were given the family names of An and Wen which are exclusively theirs to pass on to their descendants, having been naturalized in 1713 A.D. during the reign of Qing Emperor Yong Zheng;

WHEREAS, the present Premier of China, and its Head of State, WEN JIABAO, may be presumed to be a descendant of the Filipino Paduka Batara;

WHEREAS, North Borneo area was ceded to the Sultan of Sulu by the Sultan of Brunei in 1675 as a reward for helping the Sultan of Brunei overcome his enemies;

WHEREAS, in 1878, the territory of North Borneo (Sabah) was leased to Gustavo Baron Von Overbeck of the British North Borneo Company for the amount of 5,000 Malayan dollars a year by Sultan Jamalul Ahlam to financially support the Sultanate's war with Spain;

WHEREAS, in 18th century the Sulu Sultanate was the most powerful in the Malay world, with its empire at its peak;

WHEREAS, the Sultanate acquired a US protectorate status through the Kiram-Bates Treaty of 1899;

WHEREAS, commercial rivalries and the quest for colonies by the Spanish, Dutch, French, Germans and British led to the downfall of the Sulu Empire, and its incorporation into the Republic of the Philippines --

Be it then resolved, as it is hereby resolved that the Legislature of the Philippines recognize the legitimacy and traditional role of the Sultanate of Sulu and North Borneo, without in any way conceding it any sovereign power, cognizant of its honorary position and usefulness as mandatory participants without veto powers, in any agreement involving the Philippine government and the Muslim population of Southern Philippines – and perhaps promote it as our own "royalty" to join other crowned and uncrowned heads to bring pomp, pageantry and poetic fancy to an otherwise drab and prosaic world.

October, 2012

ooooo

HOMOSEXUALS

1. Homosexuals out of the closet

The subject for today is homosexuality and the male homo, known as a gay, queer, faggot, fag, fairy, queen, sward. These terms have practically changed the English language.

Gay used to mean happy. Queer, different from others. Faggot, a bundle of sticks. Fag, a cigarette. Fairy, a benign spirit. Queen, the wife of a king. Sward, a grass turf. Now they all are used to describe a homosexual, *bakla, sip-sip buto*. In Paris what is called an "artiste," in New York "le cocq-sacquér."

Homosexuals are those who are obsessed sexually with those of their own sex. Transvestites are different, they like to dress up as women, and are not necessarily homosexuals. Transsexuals are those who undergo sex change operations, A eunuch is a male whose sex organs have been eliminated. A fop is effeminate, but not necessarily a homosexual. A hermaphrodite have the physical characteristics of both male and female.

In the Louvre Museum in Paris, one sees a statue of Hermaphroditus, a beautiful creature with long hair, voluptuous breasts and a male organ, penis. Ovid writing in *Metamorphoses*, tells us about the nymph Salmacis who was so in love with the son of Hermes that she made sure their bodies became physically united. When they became one body, they were named Hermaphroditus. Legend says that anyone bathing in the fountain of Salmacis in Caria, becomes a hermaphrodite.

We write of homosexuality, because we feel it is important for the readers to know that such a phenomenon existed since the dawn of time, that in some epochs of history, homosexual love was accepted as normal and at times exulted as a higher expression of love than love between man and woman. It is time we took a second look at it, and perhaps accept homosexuals into the mainstream of our society, as they do in the USA and in Europe.

Recently in 1993, DNA studies showed that homosexuality is partly genetic and passed on by mothers. If so, it is no longer a sin or an abnormality, but a genetic trait like the color of the skin.

If most people have such distaste for homosexuals, why not remove this gene? This was what the Nazi doctors tried to do in the concentration camps -- to rid the gene pool of unwanted traits -- like Jews and homosexuals. Why not tinker with the genetic code, or perform abortions on potentially gay fetuses?

The answer to this chilling question is simple. We must not, because by eliminating the gay community, we lose too much. Gays are people like any other, with a close and mysterious bond that is based on something deeper than sex, a thriving gay culture filled with wit and celebration, a gay spirit that is indestructible even in the face of AIDS. Can we remove what makes a person gay and still maintain that unique sensitivity that has played a disproportionate role in the world's art and history?

What would the world be without its great homosexuals -- Socrates, Aristotle, Alexander the Great, Julius Caesar, Richard the Lionhearted, Leonardo da Vinci, Tchaikovsky, Oscar Wilde, John Maynard Keynes, Elton John?? To attack homosexuals or any unpopular group of fellow human beings like the Jews or the Negroes, is ultimately to attack ourselves.

2. Priest violates a confidence and lost a soul

Louie Cruz is is a restauranteur, an entrepreneur, an art collector, a socialite of sorts, and a self-admitted homosexual. He is the son of my classmate Ambassador JV Cruz, and my godson to boot. I knew him since he was a small boy, and have witnessed the uphill battle he waged against family, teachers, and friends to win respect and recognition for his way of life.

At the age of thirteen, he found out how different he was from his schoolmates in Ateneo when he began to be affected by the sight of boys playing basketball in shorts. He fell in love and eventually was estranged from his special friend. Hurt to the quick, he sought the advice of one of the Jesuit priest, a cousin of mine, Father Jimmy Bulatao SJ. When he got home that evening he was called to the room of his mother Lucy, who asked him if there was anything he had to say to his mother. Poor Louie, he put two and two together and realized that that Father Jimmy has violated his confidence (I suppose at the time, the Jesuits were not prepared to deal with problems of this nature). Well, that was the last time Louie Cruz went to church. He became an atheist.

His friend, Larry Leviste, who is a fashion designer, was studying at La Salle and had a totally different experience. He thought everyone was gay like he was, and acted accordingly. He told me he had his eye on one of my good-looking nephews,

Benjie Henares, who ran too fast to be caught by Larry. Goes to show you that every straight heterosexual boy must learn to run the 100-meter dash

Once when I was visiting Germany. I was invited by Louie Cruz to stay in his apartment. There were several Filipinos and Germans of both sexes who came to visit him, and I remember having been treated to a spectacle of fun and frolic I never saw before..... like golden showers and chocolate fudge. The former happens when one drinks too much beer, and the latter happens when one eats too much papaya.

It is said that homosexuals abound in families where (1) there is an overpossessive dominant mother, and a weak father-figure, or (2) there is a playboy macho father who browbeats the mother and openly keeps *queridas*. Check it out among your friends, you will find that playboy machos have homosexuals among their children. Several examples come to mind, but they better be left unsaid, or we'll get a beating on our donkeys.

3. Gay to Gay Relationships are preferred

In the United States and Europe and in the higher income levels of our society, gay-to-gay relationships are preferred. Indeed, in more permissive societies, homosexuals of the same sex are allowed marry, to adopt children and share properties. Filipino homosexuals, however, prefer real men whom they recruit among the young boys 16 to 20 years old, and ply with cigarettes, clothes, money, even drugs. Such relations between homos and straights are seldom permanent; so in the higher income levels, in the world of artists, actors, couturiers, and other professionals, the gay-to-gay relationships prevail.

In gay to gay relationships, there are those who play the part of a woman, and others who play the part of the man. One homosexual takes the role of the boy and the other the role of the girl. Which is which depends on who has the stronger personality. Homos therefore may reverse roles from partner to partner, depending on the relative dominance of one partner over the other. The boy is called the macho-queen, usually an athlete attracted to group sports such as football and basketball where he is in contact with other men. The girl is called the queen, who exhibits the most feminine characteristics such as limp wrists, swaying hips and a loud gossipy nagging voice. Closet queens are usually married, with children, and do their stuff on the sly.

They say Batman is a gay. A prominent psychiatrist suggests a homosexual relationship between Batman and Robin, and for a long time gays adopted him as their hero, and prompting comedians to refer to every closet queen as a Bruce. In vain was Bruce Wayne depicted by his fans as a playboy, with feminine conquests Julie Madison, Linda Page, Vicki Vale, even Batwoman, and the phantom female of "The Demon of Gothos Mansion." To the end, Batman remained a bachelor. The charge that Batman is a faggot forced the producers of "Batman, the Movie" to scratch Robin from the film.

Homosexuals exist even in the devil's world of religious bigots and among guardians of our morals. Roy Cohn, as the assistant of Senator Joseph McCarthy, went out of his way to persecute homosexuals as part of the Soviet network of spies, was himself found to be a homosexual. It is a matter of record that many Catholic priests are homosexuals who prey on young boys. Most bishops cover up the scandal and send the offending priests from one parish to another, there to abuse other young boys, a scandal that was exposed by Boston Globe, and cause a sensation all over the world.

4. Gays can't do what women do best

Among the most creative and sensitive and lovable persons are those in the movie and theater world --- who are they? Bernardo Bernardo and Freddie Santos who admit to being bisexual; and movie directors Behn Cervantes, Ismael Bernal, Maning Borlaza -- - whose understanding of the nuances of both sexes contribute much to moving portrayals on screen and stage, of the tragic vulnerability of the human condition. Fanny Serrano, the late Dr. Rey de la Cruz (mother of soft drink bomba stars), Babette Corquera, Soxy Topacio are swards who make it by honestly playing themselves.)

Macho straight actors love to portray gays, portraying sward roles in movies and television to tickle our funny bone. Such as the superb straight artists like Dolphy, Michael de Mesa, Roderick Paulate, the late Dindo Fernando, Vic Sotto, Joey de Leon, Eddie Garcia, Eddie Rodriguez, Panchito Alba.

Here we would like to call your attention to homosexuals of more modest means. They are domestics of Dasmariñas Village. I have two of them in my own household: our cook Arthur Belandres, and our laundryman, Judiwelo Rodriguez who is already 76 years old and still going strong with a mother who is already 96 years of age. Then there is Espie Gaspar, a cook of Dr. Augusto "Toto" Camara; Domingo Tolentino, cook in the house of Pacita de los Reyes Philipps; and also Alfredo "Eda" del Prado also a cook from the household of former Secretary Jose Concepcion.

These domestics have an organization they call Beautiful Dreamers, with members drawn from Dasmariñas Village, Urdaneta and Forbes Park villages, and including one from Ayala Alabang. Among them are educated professionals like Dr. A. D. Magno and nurse Vic Amistosio. These Beautiful Dreamers work for the richest of the rich. Sward Benilda Peregrino works for Merita Santos of San Lorenzo Village; Rodora Nolike for *Oh No! It's Johnny* Litton of Banaba Street, South Forbes; Edna Ycot for Mr. Danny Suarez of North Forbes; Edna Reyes for Mrs. Cecilia Mapa Manalo of South Forbes: Monet Teves for Alexander Ledesma of Tamarind, South Forbes Park; Emily Braken for Mr. Manolo Lopez, president of Meralco from Wack Wack Village; Auring Afril for Edmundo Reyes of Acacia Road, Dasma; Gemma Ugarte for Don Juan Carlos, father of the Secretary of Tourism.

Their activities include going to dance parties, ballrooms, discos, gay bars, excursions, picnics, and wherever they can meet young men. Probably the most popular venue of their parties is the house of ex-Commissioner Edmundo Reyes of Acacia, Dasma. In these parties, they dress in drag, in women's dresses, and dance with straight heterosexuals. They definitely do not have permanent boyfriends, preferring to have as many as possible at the same time. Why? because a permanent boyfriend usually becomes a lazy parasite.

How do they find partners? And how do homos get them into bed for sex? Usually one look and two partners know that an affair is about to begin. What do they do? Fellatio, sodomy -- the former (lip service or *coplang*) preferred with handsome partners, the latter (*orangga*) with less desirable ones. Most Filipino homos do not want to marry other homos as in the USA.

Do they go around with guards at the village? Of course, the swards provide the guards with company during the lonely watch. But guards harass the gays. Two of them even emptied their guns on our poor *lavandero*, shot him in the temple and in the heart, and left him for dead. But that is another story.

We hope after reading these articles, you have a better appreciation of homosexuals. What would the world be without them? They are better hair-dressers, dress-designers, chefs, movie-makers than most women are.

But they cannot do what women do best, right?
May 21-24, 1995, ISYU

ooooo

APOLOGIES

1. Pyrrhic victories are worse than defeats

QUE te envuelvas en un asunto legal en lo cual tendrias el derecho de triumfar, so goes a Spanish curse -- May you be involved in a court case in which you are sure you are in the right.

Under such a curse, people pursue court cases beyond all reason till no one wins except the lawyers. Under such a curse, instead of coming to terms with the Marcoses on their loot, we pursue a court case that won us $200 million which all went to lawyers and creditors -- and we got practically nothing for being so righteously in the right.

Under such a curse, families like the Castillos and the Teodoros quarreling over inherited fortune, would carry on an internecine war in the courts for years, until little was left to divide. Each litigant was sure that victory was his by right.

Such victories are Pyrrhic, won at too heavy a price like the battle won by Pyrrhus, King of Epirus, against Rome at Asculum in 279 BC. Pyrrhus lost so many of his men that "One more such victory," he said, "and we are lost."

Contrary to what Rina David wrote, I never courted "a blizzard of libel suits." His Immensity Luis Beltran reportedly has 46 libel suits, including the one filed by President Cory. Ramon Tulfo has 29 libel suits, and more coming.

I have quality, not quantity, only seven libel suits, including the most expensive in Philippine jurisprudence, a P240 million suit against me by Jaime Zobel; and P10 million each by Sen. Juan Ponce Enrile, lawyer Dick Romulo, Shell chairman Cesar Buenaventura and Comelec Chairman Christian Monsod.

Jaime Zobel and I figured we would rather be friends than enemies, so he dropped his suit, and I promised to give him a fair shake, keeping communications open between us, so that any misunderstanding may be quickly resolved.

Today I make my peace with Romulo whom I consider a colleague in the fight against monopoly; Buenaventura who is my favorite cousin; and Monsod who has long been a family friend through our children.

These three claim that I have libeled them in two columns in which I allegedly called them cowards and traitors. In a separate column, I repeated hearsay testimony I heard against the integrity of Cesar Buenaventura. We may quarrel over the wordings, whether or not the allegations are true or not, malicious or not, justified or not, fair or not, whether or not the three are public figures subject to legitimate criticism -- but it won't really matter in the end. They who should be my friends, still feel they have been insulted and degraded, which they do not deserve. If so, I am truly sorry, and I apologize, for they are certainly no cowards or traitors or crooks.

The three claim I libeled them in an article wherein I called them "greedy crocodiles... representing the same group of businessmen who kowtow to every president in every administration... politically insignificant, could not be elected even on a laundry ticket, and have always latched on like barnacles to politicians whom they corrupt with `retainers.' "

We have confirmed that Christian, Dick and Cesar are not greedy, do not kowtow to any president, are political significant through their various organizations, and do not corrupt politicians with retainers. Christian's lawyer is Dick; Cesar's Shell lawyers are Dick Romulo and the Sycip Law Office; and Dick is his own lawyer. None of them use politicians for consultation or court action.

Also in another article, I compared them to mass demonstrators against the bases, "It is impossible to imagine Christian Monsod, Bernie Villegas, Cesar Buenaventura, Dick Romulo leave the comfort of their mansions in exclusive villages to fight in the streets for their American masters. One thousand to your ten pesos say that these little brown monkeys have a yellow streak on their backs a mile wide, and will scot for parts unknown with their 30 pieces of silver at the first sign of trouble."

Christian, Dick and Cesar have every right to campaign for the US bases without being called traitors. They do not have to demonstrate in the streets like the people of Olongapo and Angeles City. They utilize organizations and the media, as I do; and there is nothing cowardly about that.

Cesar complains I called him a squint-eyed mountebank playing "the Old Shell Game," to manipulate the Cory government by delaying delivery and creating an artificial shortage of LPG; offering to bribe Biñan officials to allow Shell's "explosive" LPG storage tanks in their town; getting Rep. Exequiel Javier to sneak in a rider to exempt LPG from tax; launching Shell's "partnership for progress" with Shell getting richer and richer, and the farmers pushed to the edge of a marginal existence; and conspiring to transfer the petrochemical project from Bataan to Batangas to save Shell's underutilized $100 million entrepot in Tabangao.

These are based on hearsay, not hard evidence.

2. CrisCosby, DickRedford, CesarPlummer, me-Tarzan

Tom del Castillo's son watched me over TV and remarked: *"Akala ko guapo yan si Henares. Hindi naman pala."* I could have told him that myself, but children have a special way of looking at people with unvarnished truth.

In our grade school class, we get our first experience of this -- we acquire nicknames that dog us the rest of our days: *komang, kulangot, bugoy, negro, otot, baho, supot, bombay, pilay, taba, boteke, langaw, baboy, gago, tanga, pangit,* Matorco (one pimple on top of another).

It is a kind of Filipino humor that is prevalent in the provinces. Many of us, myself included, become inured to it in time, I don't really mind being called *pangit, kalbo, tanda or gago,* which I probably am. My fault lies in the fact that I assume others feel the same.

I am sure that my wife Cecilia doesn't particularly enjoy her beloved husband being referred to in unflattering terms. And I am sure that Winnie, wife of Christian Monsod; my cousin Nenet, late wife of Cesar Buenaventura, and his future wife who might as well be another cousin of mine; Alice, the wife of Dick Romulo -- who have good eyesight and see their husbands in a better light than anyone else, would resent the same being said of their husbands.

Looking through the loving eyes of his wife, Christian may be perceived as pleasant and amiable like superstar Bill Cosby the highest paid humorist in the United States today, with a tall aquiline nose, twinkling eyes and an engaging sense of humor, a sexy body considerably more lean than mine, and kind of integrity that President Cory Aquino and all our politicians trust to be fair and just in the counting of the votes.

Dick Romulo may be seen by Alice as a man of distinction, a legal luminary like Robert Redford in the movie, "The Presumption of Innocence," or something like that, with a head of hair considerably more luxuriant than mine, with the kind of integrity Filipinos and Americans alike trust when they put their legal cases in his hands.

Rags and Riches

Sir Knight Cesar Buenaventura, Order of the British Empire (OBE), wouldn't have been so honored by Her Majesty's Government if he did not look much like British actor Christopher Plummer (with the same Roman nose and a lopsided handsome smile, and with probably more teeth than I have), who played Captain von Trapp in Sound of Music; and if he did not do such a good job of managing the local subsidiary of British Dutch Shell Company. So is he seen by his late and future wife, we are sure.

And so I hereby resolve with the help of Thy grace, to confess my sins, to do penance and to amend my life. Amen.

In pursuance of which, I shall look upon these Three as their wives see them, handsome, good and great, as I expect them to look at me, not as Tom del Castillo''s brat sees me, but as my wife Cecilia does -- paragon of perfection and the mightiest and sexiest of all men, which is the truth, immune from the mighty thunder and lightning of a just and avenging God.... rrrrrr, wham, bing, bang, CRASH, BOOM!

Today I make peace with Christian Monsod, Ricardo Romulo and Cesar Buenaventura.

Christian Monsod, who served as Namfrel Chairman and a 1986 Constitutional Commissioner, easily hurdled obstacles ranged against him before the Commission on Appointments and the Supreme Court and is now Chairman of the Comelec. Christian Monsod, he was Secretary-General of Namfrel during the last year of Marcos and the 1986 snap elections. This was standing up to a dictator and making sure that Cory Aquino, who dared challenge the dictator, would have a fair chance at the polls. I was told that at a meeting with US Ambassador Bosworth, Joe Concepcion and Vicente Jayme, during the Snap Elections, Christian said, "We do not need American help for the Namfrel. If we cannot raise our own funds, we do not deserve to be free."

Ricardo Romulo, who comes from a distinguished family, was a 1986 Constitutional Commissioner and a member of the Presidential Commission that investigated the 1989 coup attempt, heads that prestigious Makati law firm bearing his name, Romulo, Mabanta, Buenaventura, Sayoc and Delos Angeles. Ricardo Romulo is one of the first Makati-based lawyers to lead the marches in Makati at the time of President Marcos to the astonishment of the crowd since his father, General Carlos P. Romulo, was in the Marcos Cabinet. Leading anti-Marcos marches was certainly an act of courage during that repressive regime.

As for subservience to Americans, the records of the 1986 Constitutional Convention proceedings show that Christian Monsod and Ricardo Romulo were principally responsible for provisions in our present constitution which insure that the bases agreement will end in 1991 and if it is extended, it will always be subject to approval by the Senate.

It further gratifies me that both Christian Monsod and Ricardo Romulo are with me on the same side of the controversy on the bases referendum. For most of the leading lights of the Constitutional Commission, including Cecilia Muñoz Palma, Ambrosio Padilla, Joaquin Bernas, Francisco Rodrigo and Teresa Nieva, opine that a referendum cannot overturn the Senate rejection of the Bases Treaty, nor can it ratify the Treaty already rejected by the Senate.

Further, Ricardo Romulo is chairman of the Digitel Corporation which is challenging the telephone monopoly of the Philippine Long Distance Telephone Company in many parts of the country with the planned installation of state-of-the-art equipment (fiber glass cables, touch tone dialing, digital switching), a project which we have long championed.

Cesar Buenaventura is Chairman of Pilipinas Shell and was recently honored with membership in the Order of the British Empire (OBE) which makes him a Knight of Her Majesty. Shell has been a valued corporate citizen in this country for the last 70 years. Judging from its investments in Tabangao, Batangas and in Biñan, Laguna Shell may stay for another 100 years.

On further reflection and in the face of more concrete information detailed in a stream of letters from people who know the three of them much better than I do, all vouching for them, I now realize that my perceptions of them have been too hasty, sweeping and lopsided, ignoring the many good, patriotic and courageous deeds that have swept them up to their present lofty stations in business. in their professions and in government service.

What I have heaped upon them were unfair, unkind and truly undeserved. I am sure they have been hurt immensely. I therefore retract my earlier statements against them, acknowledge my errors and apologize.

INQUIRER Chairman Eugenia Apostol, Editor-in-Chief Leticia Magsanoc, Managing Editor Rosauro Acosta and former Editor Federico Pascual all join me in my retraction and apology.

3. Henares apologizes to Monsod, Romulo and Buenaventura

Hilarion M. Henares Jr. Inquirer columnist in a brief statement, apologized to Christian Monsod, Ricardo Romulo and Cesar Buenaventura:

"Cesar Buenaventura has complained that I had unfairly portrayed him as wielding tremendous influence over Malacañang and is able to manipulate government decisions, as having influenced the transfer of a planned petrochemical complex from Bataan to Batangas, as having pressured Biñan, Laguna officials to withdraw their objections to an LPG plant in that town and as having committed assorted acts of economic treason to benefit Pilipinas Shell of which he is Chairman.

"In the case of Christian Monsod and Ricardo Romulo, they both have protested against my suggesting that they and their Makati business associates have been motivated by greed in their dealings, that they have been prone to protect American interests and have latched on to politicians in every regime, that they are capable of treachery and that they would cowardly run away in the face of trouble.

"On further reflection and in the face of more concrete information detailed in a stream of letters from people who know the three of them much better than I do, all vouching for them, I realize that my perceptions of them have been too hasty, sweeping and lopsided.

"What I have heaped upon them were unfair, unkind and truly undeserved. I therefore retract such statements, acknowledge my errors and apologize."

In a separate statement, the officers of Inquirer, Chairwoman of the Board Eugenia Apostol, Chief Editor Leticia Magsanoc, and Managing Editor Rosauro Acosta said: "We join Mr. Henares in his retraction and apology."
September 1991

ooooo

JUSTICE

1. I hold the record for the most expensive libel suit: P240 million

Fiat justitia, etsi ruant coeli! said the ancient Romans. Let Justice be done, though the heavens fall!

But Justice itself is elusive, subject to imperfect laws and all-too-human judges, subject most of all to the congested maze of judicial bureaucracy.

What Dante was to the 12th century, Shakespeare was to the 16th and Goethe was to the 18th, and Franz Kafka comes nearest to being of our 20th century. Writer Franz Kafka has to be re-read to be really understood; his haunting dream-like parables on the predicament of modern man often give astonishing insights.

In the story "The Trial" he wrote about a man who begs admittance to the Law. Before the Law stands a doorkeeper who said he cannot allow him in, "not at the moment," and tells him of other doorkeepers inside more terrible than he, who will keep him from going further.

The law, the man thought, should be accessible at all times and to everyone. He waits on a stool outside the door for days, weeks, months, years. At length he grows old, and before he dies, he asks the question he never dared ask before: "Everyone strives to reach the law, so how does it happen that for all these many years no one but myself has ever begged for admittance?"

The doorkeeper knowing that the man is dying, says: "No one else could ever be admitted here, since this gate was made only for you. I am now going to shut it."

Nothing could quite describe the befuddlement, helplessness and hopelessness of the common man seeking justice... and the impersonal, cold-hearted and distant majesty of the law that favor the rich and the mighty.

In the next few days we shall speak of Justice, the corruption of public officials, journalistic ethics and libel suits. And we start with a disclaimer. To keep this discussion on an even keel, we shall not to discuss my own libel suits, other than to inform you that I am not really subject to libel suits as much as people say I do. I have had only seven suits filed against me. The late Luis Beltran had about 45, and our guest Ramon Tulfo has even more.

But I hold the record for being sued for the most money: P240 million by Jaime Zobel.

That is why I resented the plan of several congressmen to sue the Philippine Daily Inquirer for libel in the amount of P1 billion, and that is why I feel relieved that they decided not to. This libel suit for P1 billion would have overshadowed the suit filed against me for P240 million. It would have broken my record.

2.   Public officials and public figures are subject to fair comment

As I said yesterday, I have to make a disclaimer: I am not going to refer to my own libel suits, those are taboo and *subjudice*, but we'll just dwell on the opinions of lawyers, in this case Atty. Lorna Kapunan, Atty. Tom del Castillo, and others.

The rule in libel is this: If a writer writes about a private individual who claims he was libeled, there is a presumption that the writer did so with malice. Therefore, the writer has to prove that there is no malice on his part. That is the law in the Philippines.

Malice is an essential and indispensable ingredient in a libel case. Without malice motivating the writer, there is no libel. Malice in legal terms means that the writer wrote an untruth, knew it was untrue when he wrote it, and wrote it to cause damage to the individual.

On the other hand, if the writer is a journalist and if the complainant is a public official, he may claim that the article involved is a fair comment for public information and in the public interest, and is protected by constitutional guarantees of press freedom. In many cases from US jurisprudence often cited by lawyers, the burden of proof then falls upon the public official to prove that there was malice. (*New York Times vs. Sullivan, 1964; Garrison vs. Louisiana, 1964; Henry vs. Collins, 1965*)

Why is there a difference? It is assumed that the public official has access to media and can fight back, also that he has much to account for to the public in general, and is fair game for public comment. Not so with the private individual.

What about a private individual who is a public figure but who is not a public official? The rule is that a public figure falls into the category of a public official. (*Curtis vs. Butts,* 1967; *Gertz vs. Welch*, 1974). The public figure must prove malice on the part of the writer.

Who can be considered public figures? Members of trade chambers, Makati Business Club, the Bishop-Businessmen's Conference and the Opus Dei CRC, which concern themselves with public issues and concerns, commenting in the press and public forums, are public figures.

There has never been any newspaperman ever convicted of libel after appeal, because the constitution guarantees freedom of the press, sanctity of sources of information, and the public right to know. Truth or untruth is neither a defense or grounds for libel. Malice or good faith is the issue, that is why it is hard to prove one way or the other, because motivation lies inside the heart and mind and is not a measurable quantity.

The law assumes that the public figures and public officials have access to the media, and can easily correct an untruth. They have hired hacks and paid pipers to trumpet their honesty, integrity and competence. A columnist can write only in his column, but a public figure and government official has access to all the newspapers. When Executive Secretary Joker Arroyo was fighting Louie Beltran and Emil Jurado, both well-read columnists, he used all the papers with a combined circulation of over a million copies. Louie had only the Inquirer, 200,000 in circulation, and he had to give Joker equal space. Emil had only Standard with a circulation of 40,000 copies. No contest. Joker won hands down.

3. Buaya, tuta, vulture, liar, crook, moron, asshole -- fair comment?

Public officials, such as senators, congressmen and cabinet members, even the small bureaucrat, whose actions affect public policy, are all subject to legitimate public comment.

Usually it is libelous to give public officials the attributes of animals, unless community standards make it legitimate comment. For example:

Buaya or crocodile has always been used to describe politicians and businessmen accused of giving priority to private gain over the public good. It was used by President Magsaysay in describing the Puyat brothers, and is a term used in every political rally.

Newsweek calls Bruce Babbit, Democratic aspirant, a "dog." President Kennedy called the American steel executives "sons of bitches." Everyone who kowtowed to Marcos, was called publicly and with impunity even during martial law, *tuta* or "lapdog."

Americans keep referring to Filipinos as "monkeys," and we in turn call them "jackals" or "vultures." We call each other "chicken" to denote cowardice.

According to community standards, giving public figures the attributes of animals, as long as reasons are likewise given and justified, is acceptable public comment and therefore is not libelous.

"Cowards" or *duwag* is likewise a term conventionally used to describe draft dodgers, collaborators during the Japanese Occupation, those who never risked their safety in the fight against the Marcos dictatorship, and those who refuse to demonstrate in the streets for the cause they believe in.

Politicians call each other liars, crooks or morons, greedy and unpatriotic, and in our perception they probably are. Public interest may dictate that they should be exposed as such, if demonstrably true.

To use as precedent court decisions in the early 1900s, to define what is libelous today, is irrelevant because community standards as to what constitutes fair comment are different in every time and place.

In the early 1900s, the Philippines was under American Occupation, and any charges against Americans were considered disruptive of public order. Such words are "*aves de rapina*" (birds of prey) were considered libelous by the American Occupation authorities. Whatever Ocampo or Kalaw said against Dean Worcester in the 1920s have entirely different connotations than in 1988, unless pro-American assholes think that we are still effectively under American Occupation.

In a movie recently there was a very impressive and brilliant legal battle fought over whether or not the term "asshole" is a word admissible in court as evidence. It is very funny and I shall write about it tomorrow

4. The difference between ass and asshole

In a brilliantly scripted movie scene, the defendant in an assault case was asked how he felt about the complainant. He said, "I have known him for over 12 years, and my honest opinion is that he is an asshole." The prosecution lawyer objected to the use of the word asshole, the objection was sustained and the judge asked the defendant to use another term instead of asshole.

The defense lawyer argued, "Your honor, there is no other word that has the exact and distinct connotation of the word asshole. Deceitful? Dishonest? Conniving? They are all close but only the word asshole can define the particular slime the complainant oozes. It is the only word that accurately describes my client's opinion of the complainant. We can actually prove that everybody thinks he is an asshole."

In the judge's chambers the argument continued. The defense lawyer argued, "Asshole, the word has a unique meaning, and my client has the first amendment right to express it." The judge said it was vulgar and obscene and another word must be substituted, "Give me a replacement, another word, and we will use it." The prosecution lawyer suggested "Antagonistic?" and the judge disgustedly said, "With all due respect, counselor, you are making the point for the defense.

"I move for a hearing on the admissibility of the word asshole, your honor," the defense lawyer demanded. The judge snorted, "What are you, a bunch of clowns? Nobody uses that word in my court!" And the lawyer said, "Okay, I won't use asshole, the word ass with do, just ass!" And the judge assented to a hearing.

The next day in court, the defense lawyer brought in a whole library of books, "The word ass, not jackass as in donkey, but ass as in asshole, appears in all kinds of literature, from dictionaries to sonnets. Shakespeare, Dickens, Hemmingway, George Bernard Shaw, James Joyce, Laurence both DH and TE, Freud, Faulkner, Chaucer -- the word ass is good enough for these literary giants, but not good enough for a court of law?" He made his point and the judge ruled that the word ass and asshole are legitimate words admissible in a court of law.

But there is a difference between ass and asshole. Anatomically, the ass is the *puwit* and asshole is the *tumbong* -- and the connotation is altogether different. An Ass is a jerk, a dolt, a fool, a dope, a nincompoop, a dunce, a blockhead. An Asshole is closer to er... a bastard, a scoundrel, a rascal, a blackguard, a villain, a knave, a cad.... but even closer to a pile of shit, a scumbag, a slime-ball, a louse, shithead, a mother-f---ker... and may be euphemised as a *sphincter ani* and a rectal dehiscence.

That word asshole has a special meaning for me. I use it to describe CIA Americans of low IQ, white trash Australians who manage sex dens in the tourist belt, foreign carpetbaggers and their Filipino scalawags, the traitors whose loyalty and allegiance is to a country not their own, and especially the crooks, clowns and morons among our legislators who abuse pork barrel funds and want foreign bases re-established. Assholes!

5. The truly cheated wait in vain for their share of justice

The President of the Philippines sued the late Luis Beltran for libel on the basis of his remark that she hid under the bed during an attempted coup. The Speaker of the House sued the Philippine Daily Inquirer for damages in the amount of P100 million for an article about his involvement in a behest loan. A group of congressmen reacting to a series of articles exposing their abuse of public funds considered a libel suit of P1 billion against a newspaper.

Imagine, one printed insult entitles the offended party to damages of an amount more than a fiscal and a judge earn in a hundred lifetimes. The offended parties, rich and comfortable in their Makati mansions, do not even get a scratch, and they want a P1 billion Band-Aid. This is stupid, cynical and offensive because it is almost a certainty that the case will be thrown out by the time it reaches the Supreme Court. It is plain and simple harassment of the poor writer.

Worse, it is calculated to clog court calendars in such a way as to delay or deny justice to the more needy members of our society.

Remember Mrs. Chita Bito who was burned by a leaking Meralco transformer, and the mighty corporate giant dared her to sue for damages. And Mrs. Anicia Mejia whose daughter Ana is dead, forever gone. She died years ago, skull fractured in a car accident when a PASVIL bus plowed into the family car at a stoplight on Edsa and Quezon Blvd. The bus company offered to pay P300,000, not even enough to pay the hospital bill of Anicia, her husband Oscar, her four children and two friends who suffered serious injuries in the accident.

And Rosario Baluyot? Sometime ago, 8-year old Rosario Baluyot was crippled when in Olongapo, a sadistic foreign pedophile inserted a vibrator into her vagina. The vibrator broke and part of it was left inside her body. She died before the case was brought to court, and because it takes too long to settle a court case, her grandmother settled for payment of P10,000.

A few years ago, a young man of considerable promise, Stephen Salcedo, went jogging in the Rizal Park, made the Laban sign and was set upon by a mob of Marcos Loyalists, egged on by a movie starlet, in front of clicking cameras, and was mauled to death. The court ordered his murderers to pay his heirs P30,000.

Think about Rosario Baluyot, Chita Bito, Anicia Mejia, and Stephen Salcedo, the bitterness and frustration at the slow pace of justice and the pittance with which they are compensated for their pain and suffering.

Then think of all the frivolous meaningless cases of libel in which nobody gets hurt that fill up the courts so that abused children like Rosario never get there. Everyone always says how terrible the court system is because it takes literally years to get a trial over. And we wonder why. Now think about it, Public officials feel insulted by fair comments on their performance as public servants. And they waste the court's time for years and years to claim astronomical damages.

Somehow we must send a message to these thin-skinned officials. Tell them that they are wasting the court's time while the Rosario Baluyots and the poor, abused, and truly cheated in this country stand in the sidelines, waiting in vain for their share of justice.

Libel cases of this sort are frivolous, offensive and conducted for purpose of harassment on constitutionally guaranteed freedom of the press, clog the court calendars and prevent the administration of justice for more important and more pressing court cases.

Fiat Justitia, etsi ruant coeli!
September 25 to October 2, 1996

ooooo

DOCTOR YES

Concept:

There is in the Philippines a surfeit of mobile phones for almost every family, probably one of the densest in the world, with a reputation for having the most text messages sent per capita. The Philippines also has one of the most ambitious health systems among the developing nations, but suffers from a lack of doctors. "In 2000 the Philippines had about 95,000 physicians, or about 1 per 800 people. In 2001 there were about 1,700 hospitals, of which about 40 percent were government run and 60 percent private, with a total of about 85,000 beds, or about one bed per 900 people. The leading causes of morbidity as of 2002 were diarrhea, bronchitis, pneumonia, influenza, hypertension, tuberculosis, heart disease, malaria, chickenpox, and measles.

Cardiovascular diseases account for more than 25 percent of all deaths." What is needed is to expand the scope and ability of our doctors to service the population.

Proposal:

We propose an organization called Doctor Yes Health Care with the financial assistance of individuals and corporations imbued with a deep sense of social responsibility. This organization with an annual budget of about Twenty Million (P20,000,000.00) Pesos will hire a staff of doctors who will accept phone calls (landline, Skype and mobile phones) from any person with a medical problem, and prescribe medicines and medical procedures. Any person with a serious problem that calls for personal attention will be directed to the nearest hospital or health center.

This will save the patient time and effort that often entails long waiting lines at the hospital and transportation expenses to get there.

To prevent conflicts of interest and undue influence of foreign governments and corporations, it is proposed that the contributing organizations must be limited to Filipinos and Filipino corporations, and without the participation of drug and milk companies.

Vision:

To establish and maintain a healthy population among Filipinos, and eventually among our Asian neighbors and in the entire world.

Mission:
To advocate, to establish, and to practice medicine, under a policy of:

1. Preventive health care by encouraging breastfeeding up to two years of age, even four years (*Apat Dapat)* and beyond, upon the option of the child, and to complement it with indigenous foods that are fresh, safe, and available at reasonable prices, instead of imported foods; maintaining a hot line for International Board Certified Lactation Consultants to advise pregnant women and breastfeeding mothers; and promoting a healthy life-style for the population.
2. Maintaining a call center of competent doctors to dispense prescriptions and medical advice to patients who are indigent or far removed from hospitals and health centers; and to arrange an appointment for any person with a serious problem that calls for personal attention, in the nearest hospital or health center.
3. Supporting the cheaper medicine policy of the Philippine government by encouraging the use of generic medicines as much as possible.
4. Supporting the aims of the Millennium Development Goals of the United Nations, and the Philippines.
5. Supporting the aims of breastfeeding, anti-drug, anti-tobacco and anti-alcohol advocates, and promoting a healthy lifestyle.
6. With the cooperation of the National Nutrition Council, the creation of a comprehensive National Diet composed of indigenous foods that are fresh, safe, and available at reasonable prices, instead of imported foods.

Goals:
To achieve for the Filipino people a life expectancy that is favorably compared to those of our Asian neighbors, among whom we are *kulelat*:
In World Rankings ranking # 1 Japan, life expectancy
82.7 years;
5 Singapore, 82.3 years;
24 South Korea, 80.7 years;

# 42	Brunei,	77.4 years;
# 58	China,	75.6 years;
# 62	Vietnam,	75.2 years;
# 79	Thailand,	74.0 years;
# 81	Malaysia,	73.9 years;
# 117	Indonesia,	69.5 years;
# 118	Philippines,	69.4 years.

NAKAKAHIYA!

To achieve the health objectives, Millennium Development Goals of the Philippines:

Goal 1. Eradicate extreme poverty and hunger.

Target 2. Halve, between 1990 and 2015, the proportion of people who suffer from Hunger.

Percent of Population, with per capita intake below 100% dietary requirement: 1991, 65.5%; 2003, 56.9%; target 2015, 34%. Percent of underweight children under 5 years: 1990, 35%; 2005, 24.5%; target 2015, 17.25%.

Goal 3. Promote gender equality and empower women.

Target 4. Eliminate gender disparity in primary and secondary education, preferably by 2005, and to all levels of education no later than 2015.

Percent Participation in Elementary Education: 2001-02, Male, 89.33%, Female, 90.91%; 2005-06, Male, 83.56%, Female, 85.35%. Percent Participation in Secondary Education: 2000-02, Male 52.96%, Female, 62.24%: 2005-06, Male 53.65%, Female, 63.53%. No problem here, the girls beat the boys already.

Goal 4. Reduce child mortality.

Target 5. Reduce by two thirds, between 1990 and 2015, the under-five mortality rate.

Infant Mortality rate per 1,000 births: 1990, 90 deaths; 2003, 42 deaths; 2006, 32 deaths; target 2015, 26.7 deaths. Under-5 Mortality rate per 1,000: 1990, 57 deaths; 2003, 30 deaths; 2006, 24 deaths, target 2015, 19 deaths.

Goal 5. Improve maternal health.

Target 6. Reduce by three quarters, between 1990 and 2015, the maternal mortality ratio.

Maternal Maternity Ratio per 100,000 live births: 1993, 209 deaths; 1998, 172 deaths; 2006, 162 deaths; target 2015, 52 deaths.

<u>*Target 7.*</u> *Increase access to reproductive health services to 60 percent by 2010, and 80 percent by 2015.*

Fertility rates: 2003, 3.5 births per woman; 2006, 3.2 births per woman. Rate of Contraceptive Prevalence among 15 to 49 years old married women: 2001, 49%; 2006, 50.6%. Unmet needs for reproductive health services: 1998, 19.8%, 2006, 15.7%. Pre-marital sexual activity: 1994, 18%; 2002, 25%. In 2006, 6.3% of women 15-19 years old began child-bearing and most of them were poor. By 2013, the Reproductive Health Bill was passed, but was challenged in the Supreme Court by the Catholic Church. The Act was suspended by the Court with Temporary Restraining Order.

Goal 6. Combat HIV/AIDS, malaria and other diseases.

<u>*Target 8*</u>. *Have halted by 2015 and begun to reverse the spread of HIV/AIDS.*

In 2006, six Filipinos were reported infected with HIV every week. One in every three cases was an OFW, mostly seafarers and domestic workers who reportedly had unprotected sexual contact. Cases among OFWs are easily detected because they are mandated to undergo HIV-testing by their prospective employers. Recent figures on HIV and AIDS cases suggest the infection has spread, not reversed. However, in spite of these new cases, the national target of keeping the prevalence rate at less than one percent of the population remains within target.

<u>*Target 9*</u>. *Have halted by 2015 and begun to reverse the incidence of malaria and other major diseases.*

Malarial morbidity rate per 100,000 population: 1998, 72 cases; 2002, 47 cases; 2005, 55 cases. Mortality rate per 100,000 population: 1998, 0.8 deaths; 2002, 0.1 deaths; 2005, 0.17 deaths.

Tuberculosis Mortality Rate per 100,000 population: 1999, 37.7 deaths; 2005, 13 deaths, 2005, 71 cases detected, 82% cured.

Goal 7. Ensure environmental sustainability.

<u>*Target 11.*</u> *Halve by 2015 the proportion of people without sustainable access to safe drinking water.*

Percent of population with access to safe drinking water; 1999, 82%; 2002, 80%; 2004, 80.2%; target 2015, 86.8%. Percent of Population with access to sanitary toilet facility: 1999, 85.7%; 2002, 86.0%; 2004, 86.9; target 2015, 83.8 %.

Goal 8. Develop a global partnership for development.
Target 15: Provide access to affordable essential drugs, in cooperation with pharmaceutical industries.

According to the WHO, only 66% of the country's population has access to essential medicines. And the prices of medicine are about 10 times what are being charged in India. Despite of the opposition of the pharmaceutical association headed by Pfizer, the government was able to initiate the Parallel Importation Program as an innovative strategy to reduce the costs of essential medicine. This and the Generics Act of 1988 enabled the government to reduce the prices of essential medicines. Assuming 2001 prices to be 100%, in 2004 it was 60.9%, in 2004, it was 41%, in 2006 also 41%, and a targeted 50% in 2015.

Strategies:

The idea for Doctor Yes originated in a conversation between Mr. Ben Liuson of the Generics Pharmacy, Inc., Dr. Elvira Lichauco Henares-Esguerra of the Breastfeeding Philippines, and her father, Hilarion M. Henares Jr. This idea will be discussed with the Public Service Station UNTV's CEO, Daniel Razon, SGV Chairman Emeritus Washington Sycip, ex-Senator Richard Gordon, president of the Philippine Red Cross, and the president of JCI Senate: and if their reactions are positive, then further consultations will be taken with representatives of the charity foundations of Metro Bank, BDO, BPI, and Aboitiz for possible financial assistance. A consortium of ten companies contributing P2 million each annually, should be enough to start the project on a viable basis.

Essential to the strategy is to secure from Smart and Globe Communications a common toll-free hot line, with a familiar number like 911 or 911-911, and from Convergys, a call center service to receive calls to the 911 number and relay the calls to the doctors in their individual cell phones, free of charge.

It is also essential that licensed doctors proficient in the major dialects be hired to answer the calls; also that the CEO of the operations have the cooperation of an organization with an outreach to the boondocks, such as UNTV Public Service which has 1,196 satellite coordinating centers, or the Philippine Red Cross, both of whom are also exempt from taxes, and free from any impositions by Revenue Commissioner Kim Henares.

It is also important to have a working partnership with major newspapers (Philippine Daily Inquirer, Philippine Star, and Manila Bulletin), major television stations (ABS-CBN, GMA-7, TV-5), newspaper columnists with a penchant for advocacies, and foreign news agencies (Associated Press, United Press, Agence France-Presse, Reuters).

A doctor should be the Chairperson of Doctor Yes Healthcare, Inc., preferably a dermatologist, because the most visible effect of any systemic disease is on the skin. A dark skin color, like the bark of a tree, betrays a kidney problem. A non-healing wound indicates advanced diabetes. A bloated face, a hump called a buffalo back, indicates extensive use of steroids for long periods of time. A pink complexion and smooth glowing skin shows a person of good health. And the skin-to-skin contact that results in the emotional bond between mother and child in the act of breastfeeding, is of special interest to the skin doctor.

Breastfeeding is of special interest to Doctor Yes because it provides the child with immunity against infections, protection against lifelong non-communicable diseases like diabetes, hypertension, and obesity. And it is the cheapest and most far-reaching strategy for the alleviation of poverty, which is the greatest problem of the country.

It is also important that Doctor Yes maintains close relations with organizations that do charitable work, like the Rotary and various groups of balikbayan doctors, who sponsor operations correcting cleft lip, and other services.... also with multi-specialty out-patient clinics, like Clinica Manila and MD Eastwood.... And with such government departments as those of Social Welfare and Development, and of Environment and Natural Resources... and international agencies like World Health Organization, UNICEF, and the International Labor Organization, which attend to issues involving women, children and specially the poor.

There will be a need to educate the people, especially the poor patients and the doctors in the use of Skype, the still and movie capabilities of the cell phone and the Pad, for use as a convenient tool for the cursory diagnosis of ailments, by the doctor far removed from the patient.

There will also be a need to get tax-exempt status for Nurturers of the Earth as the main convenor for this project, and

Doctor Yes Health Care, Inc., as the implementor of the project, to facilitate donations.

Historical Antecedents:

Virtual Doctors Project operates in Zambia, Southern Africa, where under-
age 5 mortality rate per 1,000 births is 111 deaths (Philippines, 24 deaths), and where there is 1 doctor for every 13,000 people (Philippines, I doctor for every 800 people). This project uses the local mobile broadband network to connect rural clinics with doctors around the world, for diagnostic and treatment advice, and enables medical personnel to treat patients, or offer advice to local medical staff in remote locations without needing to be present. This can either be done in real time in the form of live video conferencing or a radio or telephone link, or as a "store and forward" system where patient information is sent back and forward with comments and advice. This latter version is often more suitable in remote regions where electricity and telecommunications are expensive and often intermittent.

This project was founded by two Britishers, Huw Jones who serves as Executive Director on Development, and Peter Mustardé who now serves as Executive Director of Operations, assisted by Heather Ashcroft who helps with the Public Relations and Fund-raising. They are governed by 3 British Trustees, and 7 medical advisers, headed by and American doctor operating in the New York University, and composed of 4 Zambian doctors and 2 British doctors operating in Zambia. They may be contacted by email: info@virtualdoctors.org, and by telephone +44 (0)1273 704760.

This project relies on small donations by internetizens, an approach that entails considerable effort and expense in raising money (as against the relative ease of asking donations from Filipino businessmen. This project also relies on the cooperation of foreign doctors whose services may be very expensive (as against the existence of a good number of world-class Filipino doctors willing to help their unfortunate brothers *gratis et amore*).

Bangladesh SMS service, under government initiative, are allowing patients to reach a health worker for advice at no cost

24 hours a day, receive prenatal care reminders and even send complaints about patient care. In Bangladesh, where there is 1 doctor for every 3,200 people (Philippines, 1 doctor for every 800 people) and 1 hospital bed for every 1,738 people (Philippines, 1 hospital bed for every 900 people), and a population of 140 million (Philippines, 90 million), it is very much harder to ensure adequate health care.

Cut off from formal medical care, many patients turn to untrained or "fake" doctors, leading to fatal remedies – a situation that is being remedied by sound medical advice. There are many hard-to-reach areas where it is difficult for the people to quickly rush to the hospitals. These people are getting health advice by the mobile phone health service. Most phone calls through the free health advice hotline come in the middle of the night, said Sazzad Hossain, a medical officer, "People might have very insignificant problems but when they hear from a doctor, they are relieved." Sazzad said local leaders and newspapers have publicized the 24-hour hotline contact numbers nationwide.

Shakhawat Hossain, 30, an agricultural laborer, said health advice via phone can help when there are no other alternatives. When his 3-year-old daughter recently had a 3 AM bout of diarrhea, he was anxious, knowing how difficult it was to get to the closest hospital. "My wife told me that she had heard that anyone can get help from the sub-district doctors by mobile phone. I phoned the doctor and he told me everything I should do," he said. The health worker on the other end of the line instructed him to feed her liquids and a homemade saline solution. Within hours, his daughter's condition improved. Every year, a rural child has an average of 4.6 episodes of diarrhea, from which about 230,000 children die annually. Even though there is an effective treatment solution of salt and sugar, known as oral rehydration therapy, less than 30 percent of the patients who need it use it, and only 17 percent do so properly. Diarrhea advice by phone helps a lot.

Comparison: The Zambia experience involves doctors, the Bangladesh experience, only health workers. Zambia depends on foreign charity, Bangladesh on the government. Our Doctor Yes depends on private initiative from Filipinos themselves, and will involve paid Filipino doctors with free advice from more experienced doctors from private hospitals. We feel this is the best approach in the Philippines, given that there is no lack of wealthy Filipino individuals and corporations imbued with corporate Social Responsibility, and the knack of foreign governments and corporations to undermine public health policy when their business profits are at stake (witness the milk companies' campaign against Breastfeeding, and drug companies' opposition to the Cheaper Medicines and Generics Laws). Together with Bangladesh and Zambia, we are aware that the Information Revolution has brought us an excellent tool (cell phone) for use in our fight against disease and an unhealthy lifestyle involving drugs, tobacco and alcohol.

Project Study:

The scourge of poverty is disease. Even the most insignificant fever or pain causes fear, trepidation and stress that drive the poor into long lines at government hospitals where they get infected with even worse diseases. The thought that disease, so randomly acquired, can inevitably lead to death and penury, drives them in desperation to commit thievery and even murder. The primary goal of Doctor Yes Healthcare is to relieve this stress, this desperation, and assure the poor that sound medical advice may free them from the necessity to spend precious time and money for transportation, and long waiting lines in hospitals, at absolutely no cost. At the same time, Filipino doctors with compassion and bedside manner for which they are famous all over the world, may induce the poor to adopt a healthy lifestyle, with adequate nutrition provided by indigenous foods, locally available, not expensively imported; proper pre-natal care and breastfeeding to ensure immunity of the future generations against lifelong diseases. The secondary goal of Doctor Yes is to identify the more serious cases that need specialized attention, and refer the indigent patient to where they can get medical service and medicines at the cheapest cost.

This worthy project must be done right. First, we have for the past five years conducted a pilot project to determine the validity of our approach. At address 459 Quezon Avenue, corner Banaue Street, stands a 4-story building with a large poster of Vilma Santos endorsing generic medicines. On the first floor is located one female licensed doctor (female because most women patients trust doctors of their own gender), being paid P40,000 a month (twice what new doctors get in government hospitals), who runs the Dial-A-Doctor office from 8:30 AM to 5:30 PM. Anyone calling telephone 732-3333, is entertained by this doctor, giving sound medical advice. She now receives a daily average of 20 calls and 20 visits from patients within the area, and follows the SOAP protocol: S = Subjective Complaint; O = Objective Evaluation of the Complaint; A = Assessment by the Doctor: and P = Plan of what is to be done. The success of this pilot project leads us to the next step.

Second, we shall expand this approach to an operation 24 hours a day and 7 days a week, by hiring two extra licensed doctors. This time the doctors will be trained to encourage pre-natal care for pregnant women and breastfeeding for nursing mothers, according to protocols developed and approved by the Academy of Breastfeeding Medicine and International Board of Lactation Consultant Examiners. The venue is donated free. We shall pay the salaries of the three doctors assigned to three shifts a day for six days a week in this office, and one Chief Operating Officer (COO) at the rate of P40,000 each for 13 months or P2,080,000 a year. We will also hire 3 extra doctors part-time for three shifts on Sunday at 1½ times the daily rate of P40,000 divided by 25, times 52 weeks a year, or P124,800 plus 1/12 of that amount for Christmas bonus, P10,400, for a total of P135,200. The Total Payroll for the year will therefore be P2,215,200, for the Second Phase. We hope that at this time, we shall have been given toll-free number that is easy to remember.

The Third Phase, at this time, follows automatically hereafter. Every time a particular shift is increased by more that 40 calls/visits a day per doctor, an extra licensed doctor is hired to take up the slack. This will continue until the demand for doctors have stabilized, in which case the Fourth and Final Phase comes into play.

In the Final Phase, which may happen in the year 2014, we hope to have 20 licensed doctors at P40,000 a month for 13 months a year, a direct payroll of P10,400,000 a year. Plus a Chief Executive Officer (CEO) at P50,000 a month, a Chief Operating Officer (COO) at P40,000 a month, and an Executive Secretary at P30,000 a month, all for 13 months a year, an administrative payroll of P1,560,000 a year. A staff of three oversight members, paid at P20,000 per month for 13 months, will hired to handle complaints and suggestions – for which P780,000 is budgeted. The total yearly payroll will be P12,740,000 a year. Plus an additional P2,360,000 a year for equipment, supplies, electricity, telephones, water, car, and other contingent expenses. And an extra P5,000,000 a year to build up a investment fund to make Dr. Yes Health Care, Inc. a self-sustaining organization. This will require a yearly infusion of P20,000,000 a year, to be shared by 10 Foundations at P2 million each, whose representatives will serve in the Board of Trustees of Doctor Yes Health Care, Inc., along with one doctor representative, and three of administration staff, chaired by the CEO. We welcome 10-year pledges from 10 donors to donate P2,000,000 a year for the next decade.

The same toll-free number will be used, passed through a call center, which will relay the calls to individual doctors, each with individual cell phone numbers (supplied by Doctor Yes), each doctor operating in his/her own house or office, or even on the run. We hope that we will be able to convince Ms. Marife Zamora, CEO of Convergys Call Centers, with its 33,000 employees in 18 locations, to accommodate Doctor Yes Health Care, Inc., free of charge, with just one employee receiving our 911 calls and relaying them to all our doctors.

In the long run, we will ultimately have a non-government organization that receive 800 calls a day, or 292,192 calls a year, that will empower the poor to help themselves to a healthy life style devoid of drugs, tobacco and alcohol, and an environment that will keep them healthy and happy. All of these in the service of Pope Francis I, of God and Country.
November, 2013

END OF BOOK

www.ingramcontent.com/pod-product-compliance
Lightning Source LLC
Chambersburg PA
CBHW051745250726
48659CB00001B/259